THE HAPPY COUPLES GUIDE TO

INVESTING IN RENTAL PROPERTY

BY CHAKIB AND JINAN JABER

PICOLEE
PUBLISHING

THE HAPPY COUPLE'S GUIDE TO
INVESTING IN RENTAL PROPERTY

FIRST PICOLEE PUBLISHING EDITION
DECEMBER 2019

ISBN: 978-1-951857-00-4

WWW.PICOLEE.COM

Dedicated to our daughter Natalie and son Danny,
without whose patience, support, and love
our tasks would have been much less enjoyable.

CONTENTS

AUTHOR'S NOTE

The Happy Couples Guide to Investing in Rental Property is the how-to story of one middle-class couple who worked together as a husband and wife team to build a real estate portfolio while maintaining and complementing their relationship.

The guide gently brings readers on a journey from the idea of owning some investment property all the way through to insuring college tuition for children, having a secure retirement, and acquiring wealth. All while building a stronger relationship. Jinan and Chakib met in 1997; they got engaged shortly thereafter on Valentine's Day in 1998 and were married that same year.

They've been happily together since, and they now live in Annandale, Virginia with their two children, Natalie and Danny.

The book is an updated version of the original publication "The Happy Couples Guide to Investing in Real Estate" first published on Valentine's Day in 2013. Since then our investment in real estate has expanded to investing in land, multi units, flips and real estate based stocks and mutual funds. We truly wanted to focus this book on our rental property approach. Hopefully in the future we can share with you our other successes.

The book provides a comprehensive manual for working together as a couple to build a brighter future. Included within are ideas for:

- Investing for the future while strengthening your relationship
- Saving investment capital
- Maximizing investment returns to build a source of passive income
- Finding, structuring and negotiating great investment deals
- Renting and managing property painlessly
- Reducing cost, and tax considerations
- Leveraging each other's strengths to achieve your goals as a couple

We truly hope that you take the time and enjoy reading the book as a couple.

INTRODUCTION

OUR FIRST BABY: HOW IT ALL STARTED

It's always fun to share the story of how we first got started in real estate investment. We are a typical middle-class, hardworking couple living in the Washington, D.C., metro area. We have been happily married for over twenty years, and bought our first rental property in 2006. Perhaps we should begin with how and why we got started. We were both working and making good money. However, it always felt like at the end of the month, we had nothing in the bank to show for our hard work. We had been living in a townhouse we owned for only two years, and sold it for around $100,000 profit, which we used as a down payment for a single-family house in Falls Church, Virginia. It was the height of the real estate market and we saw the potential to build wealth through real estate. The sale of our townhouse opened our eyes to the possibilities of investing in that market.

CJ worked at Freddie Mac for several years, and before that for Reuters' investment division, which gave him an inside view into the trading and mortgage industries. Before getting into sales, Jinan also worked as a financial advisor with American Express Financial Advisors (now Ameriprise) while pursuing her MBA degree at George Mason University. With that background, we knew quite a bit about investment vehicles, from stocks and investment funds to retirement and savings vehicles.

As an avid investor, CJ started by dabbling in stock and mutual funds investments, and then he experimented with different investment trading strategies that were used at large firms and applied complex analyses to stock trading. Through the market volatility and the uncertainty in the economy, we thankfully didn't lose money. While we kept on investing in the market and leveraging financial advisors to augment our experience, we wanted to look at options to diversify our investment portfolio and hedge our risks. This new strategy included taking a look at passive income options which included real estate investments.

We started looking at different long-term investment strategies for our future, and real estate seemed like the right answer for us. We wanted to own solid assets, the kind that are likely to grow in value over the years and which don't completely lose their value should the market fluctuate. When we looked at options of getting funding to support our investments, we decided to refinance our primary house, which had adjusted in value, and took out around $200,000 in cash.

That was 2004, when real estate value had reached its peak. We used that money to finance the purchase of our first rental property. A few years later, we sold our property in Falls Church and relocated to New Market, Maryland, where we were able to eliminate our debt. We actually purchased a larger home with better school districts for our family. Today we still own the property in New Market as our family vacation home and additionally have invested in a full rehab that is our current home in Virginia.

In 2005, once we had the financing options figured out, naturally, the next question was where to invest. We started our search from a strong foundation: places we already knew we liked. Instead of taking long, expensive vacations, we enjoyed road trips that took us about two to three hours away from our home. We both love peaceful scenic drives in the country and also the time away from our hectic lifestyle in D.C. Being a self-proclaimed online search guru, Jinan started looking at rural areas we'd visited to determine if it would make sense for us to invest there. Since we had the land in Romney, West Virginia, we were very familiar with the city of Cumberland, Maryland, which was close by. That's where we found our first "baby."

What we liked about Cumberland was its scenic setting in the country, its proximity to D.C. and to the land in West Virginia that we had just bought, and its affordability in terms of real estate value. We started researching different investment properties in the area. Our philosophy from the beginning was to invest in a property where we would like to live, because we wanted our tenants to be happy. We found a real estate agent who started sending us different listings based on our criteria and budget. Even though there was no shortage of low-priced properties, we didn't find any place that we would want to live after doing a walk-through; some required major renovation work and others were rented and in a really bad shape. We kept looking.

When we did the first walk-through of what became our property on Columbia Street, we instantly fell in love with the red-brick charming row house. It was well maintained on the outside with a nice front porch. As we walked in, we were immediately impressed by the gleaming hardwood floors, large bay windows, high ceilings, and traditional fireplace in the living room. The spacious layout was designed to make it easy to convert the property into a two-unit duplex.

We talked to our agent and decided to make an offer. The seller was a motivated seller and had kept the house in immaculate condition. The property was listed under market value at $78,000 (market value at the time was approximately $86,000). Our agent contacted the listing agent to discuss our interest. We offered $65,000 for the property and we ended up buying it in a seller's market for $70,000. That was our first lesson in the real estate market: be patient and be ready to negotiate.

Next we worked with a property manager to prepare the property for rental. Virgil Twigg from Twigg Realty was the listing agent on that first property we purchased in Cumberland. He was also a property manager, and we liked our dealings with him so much that we asked him to manage the property after we purchased it. Virgil helped us understand the area's rental market. He walked us through what we needed to do to pass the inspection, how we could make the house into a two-unit property to increase the rental income, and how much we could expect to charge. His expertise was invaluable in helping us get started, and we were very excited to embark on our first rental property adventure. We continued to work with him for years. Though he passed away this year, he was a great mentor as we learned to navigate and understand the business.

The property management fee per year on our first property was about one month's rent, and taxes in Cumberland were very low compared to Washington, D.C. The property was rented within two months of our purchase.

This model seemed to work for us, and as we started getting cash from our first property we continued to look for other investments in Cumberland. However, in order to minimize our risk, we also wanted to diversify. We started researching other areas of investment and found our second "baby," a beautiful duplex in Williamsport, Pennsylvania.

When we first began investing in real estate, it was more of a dream than a well-thought-out plan for the future. We continue to purchase more properties, year after year—at the time we wrote our first book, we owned fourteen units; today we own more than thirty units and are working on a number of other deals. We love the continuous income, the peace of mind and financial security, and most of all the freedom that comes from knowing that we don't have to worry about the future, as our properties appreciate in value, generate monthly income, and provide the family with solid tangible assets that we can sell or pass on to our children. All our investing has been done in our spare time while we've both been very successful at our day jobs. Working with each other and leveraging each other's strength has been a rewarding experience; not only has it made our bond stronger, it has made our family stronger. One of the best side benefits of real estate investment has been the adventures we've had along the way. In this book we will focus and share our lessons learned in our approach to investing in rental properties.

INVESTING IN REAL ESTATE AS A COUPLE

Investing as a couple can be a very rewarding and fulfilling experience; however, it also has interesting challenges. In making any decision as a couple, there may be hesitation or fear over what's the best way to invest for your future and how to make it work; this also holds true in real estate investment. We look at our real estate investment as a business venture in which we are business partners and our decisions and approaches have to make business sense. Working as a couple and treating this as a business partnership allows us to look at investing from a different perspective. Of course, as in any business, different people have different roles, and we have been able to divide the work based on our strengths and work together as partners who share the challenges and successes of our efforts.

Before we started investing in real estate, we faced some of these challenges. As we look back at them, we realize they were mainly caused by agreeing on risk acceptance, fear of the unknown, and uncertainty.

You might face these challenges if you want to invest and your partner disagrees with the idea due to hesitation, doubt, or fear of commitment and potential risk. Our success has stemmed from working with each other and trusting each other as we worked through the different challenges. Our process over time has evolved to developing a way of open communication, outlining each other's positions and agreeing on a middle ground that both of us are willing to accept; sometimes it is Jinan's way and other times it is CJ's way. Mistakes will happen and what will measure your strength is how you handle the challenges as a team.

Since these are very common obstacles when planning to invest in real estate as a couple, it's very important to address these fears and doubts early on and to communicate openly in order to thoroughly address everyone's concerns. An approach that has worked very well for us is to identify the root cause for hesitation or disagreement and address it by talking through a worst-case/middle-case/best-case scenario. By understanding the worst that could happen before making a decision to move forward, you can address potential concerns and ensure that both of you are committed and confident in the investment plan that you develop. This is a critical success factor when you're investing in real estate as a couple.

As an example, here are a couple of obstacles we had to address (you might have similar challenges to work through):.

FEAR OF SPENDING OR LOSING ON REAL ESTATE INVESTMENT

Making the commitment to invest money (or life savings) in real estate can be intimidating, especially if you're afraid of losing your hard-earned money. However, when you look at the risk factors for real estate investment versus other investment vehicles, the risks are relatively low, since you are investing in the ownership of a tangible asset that is likely to accrue value over time, especially if you have a long-term investment strategy. To thoroughly understand the potential risks, let's look at the worst, middle, and best-case scenarios and try to address the concerns of potential money loss. It is important to take into account that your return on investment (ROI) is both the rental income that you receive each month and any change in the property value.

WORST-CASE SCENARIO

To illustrate the worst that could happen, let's say you invest $70,000 and the property value is reduced below your investment due to a real estate market crash. You might start thinking that you should have invested in bonds, gold, energy or some other investment vehicle. However, when you look at real estate investments, you need to take into account the income that you have received from the property over the years.

Let's suppose you lose 25% on the asset valuation of your property but you're renting it for $900 per month. If you follow the investment formula discussed later in this book, you will be able to recover your initial investment in seven to eight years, and you can be assured that rental income after that time period will cover the potential loss due to market fluctuation and help you make a solid profit. Furthermore, it is very unlikely that the property will lose value over a long period of time, if you placed the right offer initially for the property. With a long-term investment strategy, you can significantly reduce the risk of losing money on your initial investment. It is important to note that, to date, even with real estate values dropping, none of the properties we purchased during the height of the real estate market are under value, and they are at market price today. That is because we never paid market price and we have always been able to find properties for which we can offer 25%-35% below market price. In addition, because we pay attention to the upkeep of our properties, our vacancy rate is minimal and our tenants have been long-term tenants who consider our properties their homes.

MIDDLE-CASE SCENARIO

Let's use the same example of investing $70,000 in a rental property, but in this case the property values in the area stay the same. You will not make any money if you sell the property. However, if you're renting the property and generating income every month, you may be able to recover your initial investment in seven to ten years. So even if you sell the property after five years for the purchase price, you will still be ahead since you are collecting income on a monthly basis from your property.

BEST-CASE SCENARIO

Same example of investing $70,000 in a rental property—this time, the property values in the area go up due to a real estate market boom. You will increase your assets and make money if you sell the property. Moreover, if you're generating rental income on a monthly basis, you will increase your ROI not just with rental income, but with the actual value of your property.

FEAR OF NOT HAVING ENOUGH TIME TO INVEST IN REAL ESTATE

It takes time to succeed in real estate investment, and not having enough time to do it is a valid concern, especially when both partners are working full time and need to focus on their day jobs. This was certainly a concern for us when we started investing, and that's why we advocate securing a reliable property management company in the area of your investments. By working with a reliable and experienced property management company, you not only reduce the risk of your investment, but you can focus on your day job and family while the property management company helps manage your investments. To thoroughly understand the potential risks, let's again look at the worst-case/middle-case/best-case scenarios and try to address concerns about not having enough time. The following scenarios assume that both partners have full-time jobs.

WORST-CASE SCENARIO

We do not recommend you managing your own properties, but let's say you decide to manage your own investment property by screening potential tenants, doing background checks, keeping up with property maintenance issues, collecting rent, etc. With your busy full-time work schedules, this may be overwhelming and impractical if you don't live very close to your investment property. If you decide to take this route, you have to get organized and build a support system similar to a property management company and work as a team, splitting responsibilities and different tasks between both members of the couple based on your strengths.

MIDDLE-CASE SCENARIO

Let's use the same situation of a couple where both partners are working full-time and need to dedicate most of their daily schedule to their jobs. By having a property management company handle the daily operational aspects of your real estate investment, you don't have to be as involved in finding and screening tenants, maintaining the properties, etc. Your main challenge here is finding a good property management company that pays attention to both your tenants' needs and your own needs

BEST-CASE SCENARIO

Same situation of a couple where both partners are working full time and need to dedicate most of their daily schedule to their jobs. The best-case scenario is establishing a great relationship with a property management company you trust so that you can rely on them completely in the daily operations of your rentals, making real estate investment a passive income source.

FEAR THAT INVESTING IN REAL ESTATE WILL TAKE AWAY FROM VALUABLE TIME WITH FAMILY

Spending quality time with family is very important to us. Being a working couple, it's very hard to waste the precious moments that build a strong base for a loving relationship. What often happens when we come home after a long day at work is that we're both tired and we get so busy making dinner and getting our children ready for bed that we hardly find the time to talk to each other. During the day, we're often communicating through e-mails and phone calls. We understand the concerns that you or your partner might have about real estate investment taking away from the little time you have for your family. In our experience, however, these investments have helped us grow closer as a family. By making our road trips to the different investment areas a family affair, we have been able to spend quality time together while furthering our investment activities. Even our kids love these road trips and can't wait for us to plan our next trip.

These investments have also helped us grow closer as a couple by giving us a chance to work together toward a common goal for our future. By having a concrete goal that we both believe in, we have more hope in our future and a brighter outlook about our relationship. Our investments have allowed us to learn more about each other, and have helped us discover our strengths and weaknesses from both a business and personal perspective. The experiences and lessons learned from our investments have made us more successful in relying on each other and leveraging our respective strengths as a team to make better decisions and achieve our objectives. We believe that these investments have helped us build a future for our family, create a college fund for our children, and improve our lifestyle through the years. We feel that by following this path, we can take control of our future and be financially secure as we grow old together.

One of the great things about working in small towns is the people that we work with. We have worked with local people on a number of different projects. We have learned that the majority of folks are very open to working with young people from out of town. In addition, they are willing to share stories and wisdom of lessons learned. We have learned to take the advice of these people to heart. We mentioned our mentor Virgil Twigg, the listing agent on our first Cumberland property. Over the past twelve years, we got to know Virgil very well. We learned to trust his advice and take it into consideration when making our investment decisions. His dedication to the community, to charity, and to working hard and fair has been an inspiration for us as we keep building our real estate investments. Even with saving for the future as our focus, we have always made it part of our yearly objectives to give to charity, and just by watching Virgil we are inspired year after year.

NOTES

TASKS

- [ ]
- [ ]
- [ ]
- [ ]
- [ ]
- [ ]
- [ ]
- [ ]
- [ ]

210

CHAPTER ONE

WHY INVEST IN REAL ESTATE AS A SOURCE OF PASSIVE INCOME?

Real estate investment can help you build your future wealth and achieve financial independence.

- ☺ Real estate investment can be fun and help you grow financially strong as a couple
- There will always be demand for housing as the population increases
- Real estate accrues value over time to help you grow your assets
- ✔ A continuous income stream from rentals helps you be financially independent
- Property management companies minimize the need for active involvement
- ☺ Real estate investment helps you take advantage of tax benefits
- $ Real estate investment can provide a great return on investment
- Real estate investment helps you diversify your investment portfolio and minimize your risk exposure to market fluctuations

WHY IS REAL ESTATE A SOLID INVESTMENT?

LIFE SAVINGS

Looking into a way to secure and ensure your investments today will help secure your family's future. We needed to find an investment strategy that had been historically proven. Real estate was one of the options.

As a couple, we had always struggled to find an investment strategy that worked best for us. CJ has generally been more aggressive in his investment approach, coming from a trading background. However, Jinan has been more risk averse and conservative, seeking stability through her investments. As a couple we have always worked with each other in order to work through our decisions as a family. Most couples have probably had similar discussions or thought hard about the future and the best way to start investing. When we started looking at ways to invest for our future together, we asked ourselves a number of questions to help us get organized. Some of these questions included:

- Do we invest in a 401(k)?
- Do we invest in mutual funds?
- Do we invest in stocks?
- Do we invest in bonds/IRA?
- Do we invest in real estate?
- How do we best diversify?
- How much do we need to save?
- Will our savings be enough for us when we retire?

As we discussed these questions, we faced an ongoing challenge trying to figure out how best to secure our future. We read a number of investment books and met with financial advisors. For CJ, most of the recommendations didn't make much sense, since he had built financial trading systems and was very aware of the risks involved. Still, before we tried real estate investment, we followed these strategies for the first five years of our marriage. We met with financial advisors, followed the advice of 401(k) advisors and tried the basic strategies recommended by everyone around us. None of the investments gave us the return that we expected and that would allow us to achieve our financial goals or have a comfortable future. It was a challenge for us to determine how to become financially independent as we grew older. We were not sure what true financial independence would mean, but we knew if we continued doing what we had been doing, we would not achieve the kind of independence we wanted in the future.

As we started thinking about the people we knew who were able to build a comfortable future when they retired, we realized that most of them had invested heavily in real estate. Jinan's grandfather was a good example for us, as he had several rental properties he'd inherited from his father, and these helped supplement his income when he retired. CJ's grandfather had also invested his money in land and real estate, leaving his children with a very valuable inheritance that came in handy during tough times.

With the market fluctuation sharply affecting the stock market and our investments, especially after the "dot bomb" (the crash of the stock market and .com companies), we wanted to invest in something more tangible, more stable, and more resilient to such fluctuations than other typical investment vehicles. With that in mind, we started to explore real estate investment as a way to build our future.

Looking at ways to make passive income, we decided to explore the rental market. The rationale behind investing in rental income is that if you can find a way to make a sound investment, then your monthly return will outweigh most mutual funds, and if you invest in the right location and property at the right price, then your return will outweigh your stock investments with much lower risk. Over the years as we continue to invest in both the real estate market and the stock market, our returns in the real estate market have more than beat and still continue to exceed our expectations and planning. The trick is to buy it right and then manage it right.

THE BEAUTY OF PASSIVE INCOME

We have always discussed ways to supplement our regular paychecks with an additional stream of passive income, but we never had a solid plan before we began investing in rental properties. One of the great things about passive income is that it doesn't require active involvement in terms of management, which allows us to focus on our main jobs while at the same time supplementing our income stream. Moreover, as we acquire a certain number of rental properties, we will have the option to retire and be financially independent and self-sufficient, as the rental income will be enough to support our living expenses.

For example, we set the goal for ourselves to have the option to retire in fifteen years. By that time, we would have paid off the mortgage on the house we live in currently. Our original plan when we started investing was to have fifty rental properties generating an average of $5,000 per month after expenses. After investing for more than twelve years, we currently own more than thirty units. Today we believe our rental properties are providing us the financial security that we planned for. Based on our current expenses and taking into consideration inflation over time, we believe this will more than exceed our financial needs as we look into our retirement and plans for taking care of our kids' education.

We know several friends who have tried their hands at investing in rental properties but who gave up quickly because of the challenges of dealing with bad tenants and maintaining the properties. They would invariably tell us that the return on investment was not worth the headache of managing the property. Most of them didn't want to pay a management fee to have a property manager place the tenant, service the property, collect the monthly rent, and maintain all the records as needed.

In our experience, finding a good property management company has been one of the main success factors in our investment strategy. It's probably as important as finding the right investment properties that make our profitability formula work. Having a reliable property management company that we can trust allows us to focus on our jobs and our strategy without having to deal with the day-to-day challenges of managing tenants and properties. It's important to communicate frequently and openly with the property management company to ensure that everything is running smoothly and address any potential issues early on before they develop into major problems. If you want to get into the rental market, we would strongly recommend that you build a good relationship with a property management company in the investment area of your choice. The fee you pay will save you headaches and pain.

Today our passive income that we receive from our properties is greater than one of our salaries, which is giving us options to take risks, take extra vacations, and invest in our kids' education, as well as invest in stocks and mutual funds as part of our balanced portfolio.

GREAT RETURN ON INVESTMENT

When we started looking at different investment and saving vehicles to build a nest egg for the future, we considered the return on investment (ROI) as an important factor in our decision. We believe in diversification, but so far we haven't been able to find any investment that beats the returns we get from our rental properties.

The properties that we typically look for are motivated seller properties that are undervalued. In the past couple of years, our properties have also included foreclosures, short sales, and repos. Our strategy and investment approach has proven to work for us in any economic situation; we have found that there are always undervalued properties on the market. When we were first looking, it was a seller's market and we were able to find a property with considerable room for price negotiation, especially with a cash offer. We were able to find undervalued properties with enough research. The key was finding the motivated seller. We always thought it was important to negotiate a good deal upfront in order to make sure the ROI made financial sense; only if the numbers made financial sense did we consider going forward with a property. This allowed us to develop a profitability formula that we used to evaluate every potential rental property before we made a purchase decision. We will discuss the formula and how it works later in this book.

NATALIE'S AND DANNY'S COLLEGE FUND (ANGEL INVESTING)

As parents, we always worry about the future of our kids (angels). In addition, we are all concerned about our ability to provide financial support for our kids to get the college education they need.

One of our friends is a dentist and a real estate agent. He told us about his investments and how he has secured his future and his kids' future through the properties that he purchased. His approach to real estate investment is different than ours, and we never thought we could afford to follow what he was doing since he mainly invested in high-end properties and commercial real estate. One thing that stuck with us from our conversation was that he had returns from rental properties that he saved in an account dedicated for his two kids. His theory was that the rental income, if saved or invested in a very safe investment vehicle, would be all he needed for his kids' college education.

When we had our daughter Natalie (our precious angel), we had already started investing in real estate and were occupied by taking care of family, work, and our investment properties. On Natalie's first birthday, we got $80 from family members as part of her birthday presents. The concept of starting to invest into her college fund this early in the game became part of our discussion about what to do with the $80 we got. We asked friends and family what they were doing to invest in their kids' future. The ideas of a Roth IRA as well as prepaid education were discussed. None of the ideas made true financial sense for us, either due to the limitation on the amount that can be invested at the end of each year or due to uncertainty about where our daughter will decide to go to school in the future coupled with the low rates of return. This was a bit frustrating, since we are strong believers in education. We both struggled with managing loans to pay for our education; we wanted to do better for our daughter.

During one of our trips, we were discussing Natalie's college fund options, and it occurred to us to follow the example of our friend. We decided that the next property we bought would need to be special; it would be the "Casa de Natalie." This property would be allocated to pay for Natalie's college tuition. We wanted this property to be in an area with long-term growth. Our plan was, and is, to take the rental income and roll it into a dedicated account. Once enough income is accumulated from rent, we will either buy another property with it or invest in another safe investment vehicle. When she goes to college, we can sell the property if needed, or just use the saved money to pay for her education. One great thing about our decision was that once we told our property manager the type of property we were looking for and why, he liked the idea and was able to help us locate exactly what we needed—the property he continued to call "Casa de Natalie." The dedicated bank account has been growing and we are on our way to a substantial college fund—this account currently has more money in it than CJ had for his whole education at a state university. We are so happy with our approach for investing in our little angel. We followed the same approach when we had our son Danny. Today we have two 529 college savings plans, one for each of our children. The plans are funded from the monthly income from two of our rentals. In addition to the 529 plans, the two identified properties to our kids have increased in value and can be sold for over $160,000 to support their education, or can provide them income to cover additional expenses when they are in college.

COUPLES' ACTION SUMMARY

Real Estate Investment: Bringing Us Closer

CJ always jokes that our real estate investment has made us a closer couple and has made our relationship, love, and respect for each other even stronger. In looking at our busy lives and our friends' busy lives, we see couples struggling just to keep up with everything on their plates, and when they get home, each will focus on their own thing. Some of our friends may have a date night or a planned event to make sure that they keep the relationship going. We often hear people saying someone is married to the job, or spends more time with coworkers than family. We have seen relationships fall apart when couples fail to communicate and make time to be with each other. We always found that our relationship became stronger when we did something together that was of common interest.

Working and traveling together on these road trips, as well as managing our investments, we have learned so much more about each other, and we are able to better understand and communicate beyond just the love and attraction that we feel for each other. It has brought us closer. We have to admit it was not easy in the beginning, but with the strong base of a relationship and the opportunity to learn about each other, the road trips, the adventure, and the challenges have all been worth it to us in terms of how much closer we have grown.

If you want to get closer to your partner and get to know them better, we truly recommend road trips and working together on projects that allow you to leverage each other's strengths.

Even if you are not sure about investments, look at local areas around you (two to five-hour drives), and plan mini vacations (two to three days) to explore these areas. At least you'll get to spend time with each other and have fun. For your first task, why don't you decide who's going to find the areas to explore and who's going to plan the road trip? Go for it!

NOTES

NOTES

TASKS

- [ ]
- [ ]
- [ ]
- [ ]
- [ ]
- [ ]
- [ ]
- [ ]
- [ ]

CHAPTER TWO

HOW CAN A WORKING COUPLE SAVE MONEY TO INVEST IN REAL ESTATE?

Understanding your current personal finances will pave the way for your future investment

- Take a step back to understand your current investment strategy
- Look at your budgets to understand how much you want to invest
- Start tracking and planning
- Know your credit scores and understand what is behind your credit report
- $ Know how much you can save and how much you need to save
- Adjust your lifestyle to fit your needs
- Put in place an action plan that will help you achieve your short- and long-term goals

WHY LOOK AT YOUR CURRENT FINANCES?

SPENDING

In our house, looking at finances is always a stressful moment. It is always one person that cares about our financial position while the other just wants the other to handle it. You need to find-out who is the accounting guru in your team and decide who will look at organizing the finances.

The key to investing is developing a well-thought-out strategy, and having the funds and the discipline to invest for the future. Throughout the years, we managed our bank accounts by checking them at the end of every month and ensuring we had enough funds to save a little and cover our expenses. We also made sure that we were both contributing to our 401(k) plans, because at that time we believed that investing significantly in these plans would allow us to save enough money for our future. Over time, however, we started to realize that our investments across the board would not be sufficient for us to retire comfortably. We started discussing better and more effective approaches. This topic became the center of conversations and chats with friends. We were not the only couple with these questions. Some of these questions included:

- Will our 401(k) be enough for us in the future?
- How much will our stocks and mutual funds be worth when we get older?
- At what age will we be able to retire?
- How much can we afford to invest?
- How can we take calculated risks to invest in our future?
- Will we have enough saved for our children's college funds?
- What happens if one of us becomes disabled?
- What happens if one of us loses their job?

As we started to discuss other investment options, we had to answer the following questions:

- How much do we need to budget for our monthly expenses?
- What are we spending our money on?
- How much are we truly saving each month?
- Are we willing to change in order to plan for a better future?

In order to answer these questions, we had to divide some of the responsibilities between us and work as a team to better understand our financial position. In talking through how to get started, we identified the following tasks that we needed to finalize in order to see where we stood in terms of our ability to start investing.

- Monitor our monthly expenses
- Understand our current net worth
- Understand our current investment strategy and position
- Understand our current credit score
- Understand our current borrowing power
- Understand our future objectives and position

Jinan likes to research online and CJ likes to look at numbers, so we have divided our tasks along those lines. It took us three to five months to truly understand our spending habits. We were truly surprised when we realized how we were spending our money, and how much we could save on a monthly basis if we were willing to adjust our spending habits and cut some unnecessary monthly expenses. We identified areas that would allow us to save and have an additional $1,000 dollars in cash per month. With other changes we made, such as changing our mortgage from a thirty-year to a fifteen-year mortgage, we are saving close to $1,500 in interest on a monthly basis and a couple hundred thousand dollars over a period of fifteen years. Interestingly, we realized that we would not need to make a lot of changes to our lifestyle to save money; we just needed to make some adjustments and pay more attention to how we spent our money on a regular basis. Our objective was to look on how to reduce our spending based on our daily habits, as well as looking at our reoccurring expenses to see if they could be reduced. Areas in which we looked for savings included:

- Eliminating credit card interest payments
- Reducing car payments on loans
- Reducing home and car insurance
- Reviewing current mortgage payments and current rates
- Changing buying habits
- Eliminating as many regular fees as possible
- Re-evaluating/eliminating land phone line
- Re-evaluating/eliminating gym memberships
- Reviewing cell phone plans
- Using credit card points

TRACKING EXPENSES

From looking at our current finances, it was obvious that we needed to better understand our spending habits. This can be a fun or a challenging exercise, depending on who is spending more money. For us, as we started to look more closely at where we were spending money, we had to talk through the different expense types and discuss which expenses we could reduce or eliminate and where we just needed to change our habits.

For both of us growing up, our families truly had to manage expenses on a monthly basis and our parents did not have a lot of savings left at the end of every month. In our case, we found that some months we were saving money and other months we fell short or we barely made it.

Our goal was to save to become financially free. We wanted to aim for a secure financial future as we grew old together without worrying about living day-to-day and the fear of barely making it every month. In order to achieve this, we decided to look at ways to cut unnecessary expenses and increase our monthly savings. When we started going through this process, we were amazed at how quickly little savings added up, and this really helped make a big difference in our ability to build our real estate investment into what it is now.

Talking about money and ways to cut spending is usually a difficult topic. As you go through this process as a couple, you might find it stressful. For example, Jinan knows that when CJ is doing the monthly bills, he always gets stressed out. It's understandable because it's hard to see your hard-earned money spent quickly and on trivial things. It is very important, however, that both of us are on the same page when it comes to spending. Otherwise, we could never work toward our savings goal. In this chapter, we'll share with you some specific examples of what we did to help significantly reduce our expenses without truly compromising our lifestyle.

The first benefit of going through this process was that we were able to determine the following on a monthly basis:

- Are we saving money? If so, how much?
- Are we going into debt? If so, by how much?

This was actually a very important health check to keep us on track. It has become a way of life.

The second benefit was that tracking expenses helped us improve our spending habits. After one month of tracking our expenses, we were able to cut 25% of our monthly spending. Here are some concrete simple examples that worked for us and that you may want to look at when you start tracking your spending habits:

HOME PHONE/TV PLANS

With both of us having cell phones, we were paying for a home phone that we never really used. The only messages we were getting on that phone were telemarketing voicemails. By canceling our home phone line, we were able to reduce our monthly expenses without changing our lifestyle.

CELL PHONE PLAN

Companies are always coming up with new specials and plans to get new customers. Shop for the plan that works best for you. In our case, we noticed that we were spending more money than what we needed to when we didn't have the unlimited plans. When we also switched to the family plan (with other family members) coupled with unlimited plans, we were able to manage our monthly cost and know exactly what it was going to be. Now we are able to budget and control our monthly cell phone plans.

CABLE BILLS

When we looked at our cable bill, we realized that we had subscribed to so many channels that we do not watch. Additionally today, with so many options for monthly streaming services, we changed our packages to maximize internet speed. We got streaming services to the channels that our family watches and eliminated the cable channel package. The change to the packages reduced our monthly cable bill significantly.

EATING OUT AT EXPENSIVE RESTAURANTS

We both have our favorite restaurants, where we enjoy fine cuisine and good wine; what we didn't realize was how much we were really spending at the end of our meal, especially since we were always getting specials and discounts from the owner as regular customers. When we started looking at where we were spending most of our money outside the mortgage and utilities, we realized that were spending over $1,000 each month eating out. It may sound like a lot, but it can add up if you go out to dinner 10 times per month (twice during the week, once during the weekend). And given our family and habits, it is easy to spend close to $100 per meal—especially true today with a family of four. We had to make the decision on how to adjust our habits. That was one of the decisions that affected our lifestyle more than others. However, it also pushed us to start cooking at home and enjoying meals with our friends without spending a fortune. We now have a list of family-friendly nearby restaurants that we go to regularly..

GYM MEMBERSHIPS

We were both registered at two gyms; one close to work and one near our home. When we looked at how frequently we were actually going to the gym and how much we were paying on a monthly basis, we decided to adjust our exercise packages and memberships such that we are getting the best use out of them.

SHOPPING FOR CLOTHES

This was the area where CJ and Jinan were very different. Jinan loves to shop for clothes and buy new dresses and shoes for her, Natalie and Danny, whereas CJ could really care less if he wore the same style suit or shoes every day. When we looked at our monthly expenses, Jinan realized that she had to take some proactive measures to manage her clothes-shopping habits. She started buying more things at discount stores like Ross, Filene's Basement, TJ Maxx, and Marshalls. She also started shopping at outlet stores, where She always found great deals. For example, one day CJ got three pairs of shoes for the price of one at the Bass store at the Hagerstown outlet. A friend told us that she got many of her outfits, all very stylish, from Nordstrom Rack. We were at an engagement party once where she was getting a lot of compliments on her dress, and she said, "Can you believe I only paid $17 for it at Nordstrom Rack?" If you're really into fashion, like Jinan, you don't have to compromise style to cut expenses. There are so many options these days. Even the mall has special sales. For example, you can get a Macy's card and get regular discounts and coupons.

GROCERY SHOPPING

Prices can differ quite a bit from one store to another. By looking at weekly specials, you can save money and get the best deal on the groceries you need. We've become brand neutral as long as it's a quality brand. When there is a good deal on non-perishable items that we use frequently, we stock up on those. We know a lot of friends who love to shop at Costco or BJ's for groceries, and we used to do the same. However, since we're a small household and we were buying everything in bulk, we realized that we were spending more than we needed to and we would always end up throwing some stuff away, especially with groceries. Now, we like to shop in small portions and plan what we need to buy before going to the store. We're also lucky to have a large and diverse international community in our area, which offers gourmet foods at very reasonable prices. We always check these stores as well when we're planning to cook at home. We joined Safeway Club and CVS in our local area so we get special membership discounts, as well as discounted pricing on gas.

COFFEE

Both of us love to have our cofee. We loved having our coffee lattes on a daily basis and sometimes twice a day and definitely over the weekends. These drinks are not only expensive if consumed on a daily basis but may also have health implications. When looking at our monthly expenses, we were just surprised with our monthly expenditures. We took pro-active steps to change our coffee habit, experimenting with different home options. Today we believe we brew better coffee at home and it helps control budgets. We still indulge in the occcasional store-bought coffee, but it is all within a controlled budget.

CAR PAYMENTS

When we started looking at our expenses, Jinan was driving the car of her dreams: a beautiful silver convertible BMW Z4 with a red leather interior. She loved driving that car, which we had leased, and the lease term was nearing its expiration date. She remembers CJ asking at that point whether she wanted to buy the car and continue driving it. It was a tough decision, but we knew that the right thing to do was to look for a more economical option if we really wanted to cut our expenses. She still wanted a sporty convertible, but we knew we didn't want to continue paying close to $600 a month for her car. We started looking at some alternatives. Today she drives an Infiniti that we purchased and financed with our credit union. The car was fully paid off after three years and now we do not lease any more cars. We purchase two- or three-year old cars that have low mileage, thus eliminating/managing our car payments over time.

UTILITIES

Some of the simple things we did to reduce our utility bills included weatherproofing the house in preparation for the winter months. CJ went to the Home Depot and worked with one of the customer service representatives, who helped him weatherproof the house. Our heating bill during the winter was reduced by an average of $150 per month.

CREDIT CARD POINTS

We buy everything we can with our American Express and/or high cash-back Visa, knowing that we will pay the full amount at the end of every month. It is important to note that we don't carry any credit card debt and we don't believe in having any credit card debt. In fact, all our credit cards have auto payment set up, to fully pay the amount out of our bank account at the end of each month. If you are going to use this approach, discipline and managing expenses become extremely important. That is, you do not spend what you do not have. Currently, we can get back 3% to 6% on anything we spend on the card through reward points and cash back. We mainly use our points to get gift certificates to stores where we shop regularly or to pay for expenses on the credit card eraser tools. In fact, we look at it as if we are making at least 3% back on our money. For example, when we purchased our washer and dryer set from the Home Depot, we had earned around $600 in credit card points and we applied that amount toward the purchase so we didn't have to pay it out of pocket. We use the credit card whenever possible, especially for travel and big expenditures, to accrue reward points/cash back over time.

UNDERSTANDING YOUR CURRENT PERSONAL FINANCES

When applying for a bank loan, one of the first steps that banks require you to complete is a personal financial statement. The personal statement forces you as a couple to look at your current savings and investments (assets) as well as what you currently owe (liabilities). By looking at the difference between your assets and liabilities you develop a better understanding of your current financial position. By looking online, CJ was also able to find a number of resources that helped us track and analyze our current net worth. A good example of a personal financial statement can be found on the website of the U.S. Small Business Administration (SBA); search the web for "SBA Personal Financial Statement." You can also find a wide range of personal finance/budget planning tools online or you can ask your accountant for advice and support in the planning process. This process may take time, but it is a great way to help you inventory, track, and manage all your assets and liabilities.

ZERO CREDIT CARD BALANCE AT THE END OF EACH MONTH

When looking at credit card interest, for the majority of credit cards, you can avoid paying any interest at all. The trick is to pay for all your new purchases for each one of your statements. If you pay the full amount each month, you basically are getting a grace period to pay what you owe and you can get points or cash back on your expenditures. This typically does not apply to cash advances. It requires a lot of discipline and attention to detail to ensure that you do not carry debt.

If you do not pay what is owed at the end of each month, then credit card debit can be very expensive and on average carries interest rates between 12.99% and 34.99%. We focused some of our first efforts to eliminate our credit card debt and today all major credit cards allow you to schedule your auto payments online. For any credit card we always make sure we schedule our auto payment to be paid in full at the end of each month with a draft from our bank account.

Depending on your credit score, you should shop around and fully understand what your credit card offers you in terms of points/cash back and what the interest rate is in case you do not pay in full after the first month. Please do not consider credit card debt an option for investment down payments unless you have the funds to cover in the bank.

UNDERSTANDING YOUR CURRENT CREDIT REPORT AND HOW IT WILL AFFECT YOUR BORROWING POWER

Credit scores are the basis for your borrowing power. Credit scores range between 300-850, with a credit score of 700 or above generally considered good. There are many factors that affect your credit score and it is important that you have an understanding of credit scores. You have a wealth of online information that can help you understand your score and how to improve it. There are even some free online tools that allow you to access a credit report once every year. The credit report will show you what lenders can see when they're evaluating your qualification for a potential loan. That's why it is very important to take a close look at your credit report and address any outstanding claims that might prevent you from getting a loan or mortgage to finance your investment properties. Lenders use this information and your income to determine your credit worthiness and decide whether to grant you a loan.

You can get free annual credit reports for Equifax, Experian, and Trans-Union. Our current credit card offers free credit score and reports that we can access anytime online and it provides free credit score monitoring with alerts. You should look at your options and maybe even purchase a report to see the full details. It's always a good idea to get a credit report and check it for accuracy, especially since identity theft is on the rise. It's relatively easy and cheap to do this.

THE POWER OF BEING FRUGAL

Being frugal has always been a way of life for us. As we were looking at our future investment, we realized that we'd veered off our regular path of being frugal in a few ways—for a couple of years, we splurged a bit on dining out and leased an expensive car—but overall we maintained our trend. Still, we knew we had to get fully back on track. We understood the power of being frugal and the power of saving money early on in our lives. We are not the only ones—some of our friends are frugal like us and they plan and budget for everything. They have different investment strategies than we do but they are equally successful in planning for their future. We believe that being frugal truly pays off.

TAKE CONTROL OF YOUR FINANCES

We have talked about our situation and how we have worked to define and since the publishing of our first book, it is amazing how many folks have shared with us ways in which they have achieved saving through planning. As an example, some plan their vacations for the year in January and take advantage of early bookings. Others have found innovative ways to save on daycare, while others have found new ways to save that work specifically for them. We encourage you to look at your expenses and explore ways that work for your family, to create saving while still meeting your needs and objectives.

COUPLES' ACTION SUMMARY

One of the first steps you need to take as a couple when making the decision to move forward is to determine the source of funding for your investment strategy. This will require a proactive analysis of your current situation and doing a little planning for your future. We believe in our success and believe you can be successful.

We recommend you start by taking the following steps:

- $ Make a commitment to take proactive steps to control your expenses and plan for the future
- ☺ Believe in your goals and understand that it will take planning and time to achieve them
- Make it a goal to invest in real estate; you are not the first, and many others have done it

As a couple, it is always tough to decide where to cut expenses. Each one of us has our favorite activities and/or products. Sometimes we do not agree on what to cut out. By working together, we have learned to compromise and try to find the middle ground. We try to alternate spending on our favorite products or activities on a monthly basis so that we cater to both of our preferences. For us, nothing is set in stone—we expect to have differences in opinion.

One of the major expenses most couples have is credit card debt. You will need to eliminate your current credit card debt—this may be your first and most important step. Decide who will review the current credit card debt and who will put a plan in place to ensure that you have no credit card balance at the end of each month.

Plan on working together and remember that you are a team and have similar objectives in the end—a smile, a rose, dinner, etc. will go a long way toward resolving issues and ensuring everyone is happy with your decision as you move forward.

NOTES

NOTES

TASKS

- [ ]
- [ ]
- [ ]
- [ ]
- [ ]
- [ ]
- [ ]
- [ ]
- [ ]

CHAPTER THREE

ROAD TRIPS: HOW TO RESEARCH DIFFERENT AREAS

Road trips are fun for the whole family and they are a necessary step when assessing an area's investment potential

- $ Determine whether the area is affordable and look for available properties
- Look for a real estate agent and property management companies in the area
- ? Understand the different factors that will determine your investment success
- Understand the different factors that will affect your profitability
- Visit the area and stay there a few times before you buy
- ☺ Make it fun—make sure you like the area you're investing in
- Make sure the area is not too far from where you live

HAVING FUN! MIXING BUSINESS AND PLEASURE

ROAD TRIP

Taking road trips together is a couple's adventure. Being together without other distractions in the car for hours has helped us strengthen our relationship and brought us closer through open communication.

One of the most enjoyable things about real estate investment is that it allows us to spend time together doing something that we both like. Our relationship as acouple has grown stronger as we work closely together, leveraging each other's strengths to build toward our future financial goals. More importantly, these investments have added so much fun to our life. We enjoy all the road trips in the countryside to visit our investment properties and look for new ones. For us, these road trips are an escape from everyday life and give us time to connect and talk in the car while enjoying the scenic drives, stopping along the way in charming little towns, shopping at country stores, and meeting great people. We've always had a great time and many adventures along the way as we stop in different towns, take our daughter to discovery museums, stop by antique shops, and explore attractions along the way.

Rather than spending your weekends at home with everyone on their laptop or focusing on their own interests, you can find ways to have fun together as a family. Even as a couple, we love spending time in the car, exploring different areas and staying at hotels. These adventures really add spice to our lives and give us a chance to share our thoughts and feelings over long talks as we're driving, especially when our children are with us.

As we drive to the different investment areas, we discuss the process of finding new investment properties, assessing their potential, negotiating the best possible deal, and providing a nice place for our tenants to live. We go over where we are financially and how we need to grow to reach our goals. Throughout this process, what has helped us tremendously is that although we are very different in the way we think—CJ being an engineer and Jinan the creative type—we both agree on the end goal and the overall investment strategy. CJ is very good at developing a long-term strategy and doing the thorough financial analysis to ensure the profitability of our investments. On the other hand, Jinan uses her skills to research and find new properties, and her imagination to assess their rental potential and come up with creative solutions to address practical short-term issues.

HOW TO RESEARCH DIFFERENT AREAS

Researching the different areas where you want to invest is one of the first steps you need to take once you have decided to invest in real estate. In many ways, finding the area you want to invest in is a subjective process because it depends on where you live, as well as your preferences in terms of what type of areas you'd like to visit regularly. For example, we have always been drawn to the country, and most of our investments have been in suburban country areas like Cumberland, Maryland, and Williamsport, Pennsylvania. That being said, there are several factors that need to be researched and taken into consideration before you make a decision on whether or not you would want to invest in a given location.

AFFORDABILITY INDEX

Jinan has always loved using her research skills to look for and assess different areas for investment. Ever since we started investing, we wanted to make sure that we were putting our hard-earned money in relatively secure areas and that we were not putting all our eggs in one basket. In real estate investment, diversification is very important to protect against the potential risk of one area getting hit hard by economic downfall or natural disaster. So what is the first step to find potential areas of investment? For Jinan, the first list she checks is the affordable housing index, which is published by the National Realtors Association. It's a good starting point because it's based on the average home price and average household income in different areas. When we look at this report, we can gauge how much upfront investment we would need to invest in a certain area. There are several publications and magazines that rely on the affordable housing index and report on it. For example, *Forbes* magazine publishes a list of the top ten best affordable places to live. Cumberland, Maryland, which is one of the major areas where we invest, was listed this year as the third most affordable place to live in the United Sates. The list from *Forbes* magazine also takes into consideration other factors, such as crime rate and local school ratings, when looking at the best affordable places to live. CNN Money generates several other lists that might also be interesting when you are researching different investment areas. You can check our web site (TheHappyCouplesGuide.com) for more information and links to the different reports and lists mentioned here.

DRIVABILITY

Once you have narrowed down the list of areas you might want to invest in based on the affordability index and related reports, the next step is to figure out which areas are within drivable distance from where you live and work. This is really important, since we believe strongly that if you want to be successful in real estate investment, you have to visit your properties often and you have to know first-hand how the area is trending by staying there, interacting with the local community, and following local news. As an example, we don't like to invest in any area that is farther than a four-hour drive from where we live and work. This gives us the opportunity to visit our areas of investment frequently on weekend trips. The other strategy that we try to follow is to have our investment areas mapped out along the same driving route or within a four-hour drive from each other.

AVERAGE RENT

Once you have narrowed down the list of potential areas you might want to invest in based on the affordability index and drivability, the next step is to figure out the potential income from each area. In order to do this, you can research the average rent for the different areas. What we typically do is check out local classified ads for each area. We also check out Craigslist and look for available rentals as if we were searching for a place in the area in order to understand the competition in that market. The other source we always check—and where we usually start—is www.City-Data.com. This site provides important information about each location, including the average rental income for a condo or single-family house. Understanding the average potential rent in the area is really important when determining whether a property in that area can be a profitable investment for you. We typically look at the average home price and average rent for the area and apply our secret profitability formula, which we will discuss later in this book, to see if we would want to further consider that area for investment.

RENT VERSUS OWNERSHIP RATIO

One of the other factors we typically consider once we have narrowed down the list of prospective investment areas is the ratio of rentals versus owner-occupied properties in the area. This is an important factor because it can indicate whether there is high demand for rental properties. When you check the different indicators for the area on City-Data.com you can easily find the specific indicator to help you determine rental demand for different areas. The other factor to consider along those lines is the vacancy rate for that area. We typically gauge this based on the classified ads for rental listings in the area, as well as feedback from the property management company.

POPULATION TRENDS

Population trend is another indicator that we always look at to understand where the area is heading. If the population in that area is shrinking at a significant rate, it may be a bad sign for rental investments because there will be less demand for rentals. When looking at the overall population trend, you should consider: even if the area is facing an economic hardship, are there any signs of potential recovery? For example, one of the reasons we decided to invest in Williamsport, Pennsylvania, was that a significant source of natural gas had been discovered in the surrounding area and was attracting energy companies and employees to Williamsport, even though the local economy was experiencing a downward movement.

To understand population trends in different areas, you can check City-Data.com, as well as follow local news about the area. It's also important to visit the area during a work week and weekend and to observe local activities and events. If the town is busy and bustling, it's a good sign. If you feel like it's pretty much empty and there isn't much to do, you probably don't want to invest there.

CRIME INDEX

One of the most important factors to look at once you have narrowed down your list is the crime index for the area. If it is significantly higher than the national average, it might spell big trouble for your investment. In order to understand the crime index in different areas, you can check City-Data.com, as well as local police news. Another important way to understand the overall safety of the area is to visit and stay there. We always talk to a local real estate agent for help gauging the different neighborhoods in the area and staying away from neighborhoods generally deemed unsafe. In some cases, we have visited potential investment areas and found the situation on the ground to be really bad. For example, if you see that most houses are boarded up and the real estate agent tells you it's not safe to leave your vehicle parked on the streets because there have been recent thefts of wheels and copper pipes from homes, you probably wouldn't feel safe staying there—and neither did we. That's why we stayed away from that area even though it met all the other eligibility criteria for a good investment property. It's always been our philosophy to only invest in areas where we would like to live; otherwise, it's just not for us. This has always worked for us far.

QUALITY OF LIFE

Since we only invest in areas where we would like to live and even eventually retire, quality of life is a very important factor in determining our areas of investment. What we look for generally is the availability of good nearby health care services, easy road accessibility to shopping, good community services, nearby natural parks, and good school systems.

POINTS OF INTEREST

When analyzing potential investment areas, one of the things we always look at are the different points of interest that might attract visitors and potential tenants to move to or rent in the area. These can include but are not limited to universities, colleges, schools, hospitals, amusement parks, antique shops, farmer's markets, retirement centers, prisons, government or military bases, major industry or manufacturing, and major commercial or transit hubs.

AVAILABLE FORECLOSURES AND AFFORDABLE PROPERTIES

Once we have narrowed down the list of potential investment areas to two or three, the next step is to research the local real estate market for good deals. In order to do so, we check local listings on real estate sites such as Remax.com and Zillow.com. This gives us a good idea of the availability of foreclosures, short sales, bank-owned properties for sale, and other such investment deals in that market. We then put together a list of the properties that seem to be interesting and contact the listing agent for additional information. Once we have built a good rapport with a local real estate agent we plan a trip to the area and schedule a walk-through of the different properties we're interested in. We've never bought a property without looking at it and walking through it, and we think that's an important point to keep in mind as you grow.

GOOD PROPERTY MANAGEMENT COMPANIES

Whenever we're planning to visit a new potential investment area, we always research property management companies ahead of our visit. This is really important for us because we will not invest in an area if we can't find a good and reliable property management company to manage our investment while we're working remotely. We can't emphasize this enough, but we have steered away from investing in a couple of areas that made sense for us from an investment standpoint simply because we couldn't build a good working relationship with a local property management company to rely on for the daily maintenance and operation of our rental investments. This is a critical factor for us, as it can determine the success or failure of our investment. As a couple, it's important to divide up the tasks when you're doing all this research and determine who's going to find, contact, and build a relationship with local property management companies in the areas you might want to invest in.

AFFORDABLE CONTRACTORS

Another important factor to consider is the availability of good skilled labor at affordable rates. On one of our properties in Wiliamsport, when we were doing a major remodeling project, we were taken aback by the high hourly labor rate quotes that we got. In general the labor rates and costs of renovation will be one of your major expenses down the road in managing your property.

Before you invest, try to get a general idea of the local hourly rates for general contractors. Even if you don't need to fix your property in the short term to get it rented, you will undoubtedly need to have continuous maintenance if you plan to keep your property based on a long-term investment strategy. The best-case scenario is when the local property management company that takes care of your rental properties has established relationships with good contractors in the area so that you don't have to worry about this, but that typically comes with time, after you have built a trusted relationship with your property management company.

LOCAL CITY, COUNTY, AND STATE LAWS AND TAXES

When analyzing potential investment areas, one of the important deciding factors is the rental law governing that area. As you start looking at the laws for different states, you will realize that some are landlord-friendly, whereas others tend to mostly side with the tenant. This is very important, especially in a case where the tenant fails to pay their monthly rent and you have to deal with the eviction process. In fact, we've decided to stay away from certain investment areas for this reason specifically. CJ had a rental property in New York even before we were married, but it was mainly a nightmare for him. The tenants didn't pay their monthly rent for over five months and they were able to stay in their apartment while CJ had to go through lawyers and a lengthy eviction process to get them out. In the areas where we invest now, we make sure the laws are landlord-friendly. For example, in Cumberland, Maryland, you can begin the eviction process as soon as the rent due date has passed and the tenant has not paid the rent, and, in most instances, the tenant can stop the eviction any time before the sheriff actually comes to evict them by paying the rent that is owed. The process is straightforward and can be accomplished within thirty days.

Another important deciding factor is local taxes. High city and school taxes can negatively affect your bottom line. Since you're in this to build wealth and generate monthly income, you'll probably want to look for low tax areas for investment. We didn't quite understand the importance of this until we started to see the difference in the net monthly income from our investments in two different areas. Our property in Williamsport, Pennsylvania, was generating good monthly income; however, the net revenue was lower than what we would have gotten from a similar rental in Cumberland, Maryland, because of high school and city taxes in Pennsylvania. This gap in net revenue you're bringing in every month based on the different tax rates in two potential areas of investment can make a huge difference in your return on investment in the long run.

PERSONAL PREFERENCE

Finally, one of the most important factors to consider before you invest in any area is your personal preference. It's hard to explain a process for this step, as it is very subjective and will differ from one couple to another. However, we found that what truly kept us going in our investment strategy was that we had invested in areas that we liked to visit often and where we enjoyed staying. Again, these are areas where we would like to live, vacation, or even retire in the future.

PLANNING YOUR TRIP

CJ usually leaves planning the road trip to Jinan, since she loves to research different areas along the way and always has fun with it. On the other hand, she usually leave the driving to him, as he enjoys that much more than she does.

As a first step, decide who wants to take on this task based on who usually likes to plan, and then let the fun begin!

One thing to keep in mind is that to really enjoy a road trip, it's nice to explore the different areas you drive through and to make spontaneous stops where you see something of interest, such as a big flea market or a farmer's market, for example. That's how we keep it interesting. Every time we go somewhere, even if it's to the same place, it's a different and new adventure. With thought, preparation, and consideration, a road trip can be one of the most romantic getaways you'll ever take. Once you and your partner have discovered your preferences for traveling together, you'll have endless opportunities for more adventures.

To help you plan your road trip, here are some simple steps you may want to follow:

LODGING

One key to a successful road trip is to plan ahead of time where you're going to spend the night. There's nothing worse than having to look for a vacant room in a hotel when you're tired after spending hours on the road. This happened to us one time when there was a major event in Cumberland, Maryland, and we couldn't find any vacancy in the local hotels. We ended up staying in a very shady motel outside the town. Try to make your reservations in advance whenever possible to avoid this type of situation. This is especially important if you're traveling with kids.

As frequent travelers, it's also important to look into ways to save money on your hotel stay. Consider making your reservations online at Hotels.com, for example, where you get one free night's stay for every ten nights you book. If you have a preferred hotel chain, several of them now offer programs and special discounts. All you have to do is sign up. Try to bargain and ask for rebates: AAA, AARP, government employee, coupons.

When we get to a hotel or to a visitor center, I always make it a point to get the local attractions magazine they usually have in the lobby. These generally include valuable discounts and coupons for local attractions, as well as great ideas for places to visit while you're there.

ITINERARY

Even though spontaneity and adventure are key factors to having fun and enjoying the road trip, it's important to have a high-level itinerary to make sure you get to your appointments with the property management company, contractors, or anyone else on time. In addition, it's important to make sure you get enough sleep and you don't get too hungry along the way, as that tends to make people grouchy.

When putting together a high-level itinerary for your road trip, here are some things to keep in mind:

FAMILY GROWTH
You have a new addition to the family, but the current house is too small

SCHEDULED APPOINTMENTS
You should never forget that the main reason you're taking this road trip is to advance your real estate investment efforts. As such, you need to make sure that your schedule revolves around the appointment that you have planned for that trip. This should include planning the departure time from home to make it to your appointment on time.

FOOD STOPS
Make sure you plan for food and rest stops along the way. It's important to take a break, refresh, and re-energize. Even if you're taking snacks with you in the car, it's still a good idea to make at least one pit stop along the way to stretch and freshen up. This is especially important if you have a child traveling with you.

NAPTIME
If you're traveling with a child, try to plan the road trip around their naptime. Our daughter has always loved to sleep in her car seat ever since she was a baby, and she still really enjoys it now that she's three. We plan our appointments around her nap schedule to make sure she's comfortable. We've even set up a DVD player and some books and toys for her in the back seat so that she always has fun in the car.

FUEL UP

Keep an eye on the gas and make sure you fill up when you see a gas station if you're getting close to an empty tank. You don't know when you're going to hit the next station.

FUN STOPS AND ATTRACTIONS

So much information about little-known destinations and attractions is now available to help you get the most out of your road trip. When you're planning, it's important to consider everyone's different interests. Make the trip fun for everybody by catering to what they like to do. For example, one of the stops we always make is in Hagerstown, Maryland, where our daughter loves to visit the Children's Discovery Museum. Find out the major attractions on your way and where you're staying, and plan to stop at a couple of them to make your trip more enjoyable.

Food tips: Here are some ideas for snacking and eating well on the road.

PICNICS

You can pass a grocery store on your way and plan a picnic. Better yet, research ahead and try to find a local farmer's market on the day you're driving. Buy all the fresh local produce, jams, bread, and cheese your heart desires and then enjoy all that goodness in the park.

SNACKS

When you have a child with you in the car, it's always important to pack some snacks and drinks for the road. We always take plenty of water bottles, individual juice boxes for Natalie, bananas, a box of blueberries or blackberries, dried apricots, and raisin bread. I also often take some cooked plain pasta or macaroni and cheese for her, depending on when we're leaving. Sometimes I also make sandwiches for us that I keep in a small cooler.

☺ **LOCAL RESTAURANTS**

One of the most enjoyable ways for us to explore a new area is by visiting local restaurants and getting a taste of the regional specialties. It's so much more interesting and memorable than going to a franchise restaurant. I always try to seize the opportunity to try local cuisine by researching restaurants ahead of time and reading some reviews on Yelp.com and similar sites.

To help you plan, here are some special-interest categories you may want to think about:

- Arts (theatres, galleries, small-town charm, etc.)
- Outdoor (biking trails, amusement parks, river tours, etc.)
- Historical (historic sites, monuments, museums, etc.)
- Shopping (flea markets, outlets, antique shops, souvenirs, etc.)
- Dining (restaurants, farmer's markets, picnics, etc.)

COUPLES' ACTION SUMMARY

Decide who's going to research the different areas of investment and who's going to contact real estate agents and property management companies.

Don't let life-changing events deter you; even if you're pregnant or have a young child, make the road trip part of your life and think of it as a mini vacation.

Be adaptable and willing to explore new adventures. Have fun!

Listen to each other and keep an open mind as you talk about your strategy. When talking about the activities on our road trips, we always try to ensure that we have activities planned that meet both our interests. We have realized that while some activities may be of high interest to one of us, they may not be equally interesting for the other. Over time we have learned to appreciate each other's interests, though it took time, patience, and willingness to give new things a try. We have learned to take the same advice that we give to our daughter: when we see her hesitating, we typically tell her, "Try it, you may like it." We have taken this to heart on our road trips and in exploring new areas.

When planning you trips, enjoy the attractions in different areas: go to the park, go to local restaurants, mingle with the locals, find and explore different areas of interest. If your kids are traveling with you, make sure you plan activities that they enjoy as well—take them to the swimming pool, the zoo, or the park, and make sure that you respect their schedule and naptime.

continued

COUPLES' ACTION SUMMARY

Once you decide on an area:

- You need to become knowledgeable about the area that you want to invest in; online resources are great, but you also need to visit the area and get to know the people there.
- You need to stay up-to-date with local news. See what resources are available, online or in publications. You can't just invest in the area and forget it.
- Every time we visit an area, we stop outside a real estate office or hotel lobby and pick up the local house-for-sale listings. It's important to continue understanding the local markets. We have found that sometimes the listings are different than the ones we find online and they make for good conversation over lunch or dinner.

NOTES

NOTES

TASKS

- [ ]
- [ ]
- [ ]
- [ ]
- [ ]
- [ ]
- [ ]
- [ ]
- [ ]

CHAPTER FOUR

UNDERSTANDING WHY PEOPLE ARE MOTIVATED TO SELL: HOW WE LOOK FOR GOOD DEALS

Life is a continuous cycle—we all have changes in our lives that we must deal with

- Sellers can be more motivated to negotiate when they are under time constraints
- Life-changing moments can mean more room to negotiate: marriage, divorce, a new family addition, relocation because of job or school, the loss of a job, death or inheritance
- $ When cash flow is an issue and sellers risk defaulting on their loans, you can negotiate a good purchase price
- Repo properties owned by banks can be great way to get excellent deals on your investment properties
- ✔ As a general rule, we don't buy our investment properties from investors

UNDERSTANDING THE NATURE OF REAL ESTATE SELLING: FINDING THE MOTIVATED SELLER

REFINE YOUR SEARCH

Once you understand why people sell, you can look for specific properties that have indications of a sense of urgency or abandonment. This will help you better structure your deal.

Over the years of buying properties we have realized that people sell their homes for many reasons. In our opinion, the purchase of our first investment properties were not truly based on an understanding of why people sell, but based on the traditional approach to purchasing a property based on current market value. In our opinion, most buyers have constraints on where they want to live and have other considerations beyond market value that would be driving factors in the purchase price—buyers might purchase a property to be close to schools in the areas, because of an open layout, etc. We do not call this type of purchase investment buying, but instead, personal buying.

With investment buying, you have the time to and option of looking at different properties, since your personal requirements don't factor into the purchase decision. However, you do need to ensure the investment property you purchase falls within the right investment parameters, as defined in your investment strategy. That being said, understanding why people sell their properties allows you to ask the right questions and look for signs that you might be pursuing a promising property. Additionally, you need to be able to reduce and control the purchase price in order to maximize your profits. Instead of thinking that people sell because they are under duress, we believe you need to find motivated sellers; because of this motivation, the seller may be willing to sell the property at a lower price.

What does "a motivated seller" mean to us? A motivated seller is someone who needs to sell based on the current circumstances of the owners' personal lives, or the personal lives of business drivers if the property is a business or owned by a bank. In order to truly understand whether a seller is motivated, you need to understand the circumstances of the sale. You may need to do some digging around to truly understand the reason, but as a real estate investor it's important to figure it out.

We do not view finding motivated sellers as a form of taking advantage of other people's situations; we look at it as part of the cycle of life. Some of the reasons behind motivated sales include the following:

THE ESTATE PURCHASE

Many properties are owned by an estate. Our second property had been owned by a family for around thirty-five years. The property was fully owned with no mortgage and the kids had all moved away. The mother and father were living on the property until the father passed away. After the father died, the mother moved from Maryland to North Carolina to live with one of her children. The property had been on the market for about a year, and it wasn't well maintained. When we did a walk-through of the property, we noticed that the bathrooms were extremely outdated and the house definitely needed to be updated to a more modern look and feel. In addition, the grass was not fully mowed. It was hard for the family to maintain the house while living remotely, and they were incurring monthly costs for maintenance, insurance, etc. The kids had no intention of going back to Maryland and they wanted to sell the property. As I recall, the property was listed on the market for $75K; we offered $50K, and we invested in updating the bathrooms and overall décor (around $7K) of the property. We currently make $885 per month on the property in rental income. This was a win-win for all.

CASH FLOW ISSUES AND MANAGEMENT

- Seller desperate for cash
- Seller who can't meet payments
- Seller who needs to meet other expenses
- Loss of job/reduction of overhead and credit
- Bank-owned/investor-owned property disposal
- Asset reallocation of an investor

Example: Millionaire's Row—emotional purchase (bad investment)

To illustrate the bad investment category, I can tell you about one that we made early on. The Williamsport property was charming, with a lot of character, and on an historic street called Millionaire's Row. We had looked at other properties on that street, but they were beyond our means and didn't fit into our investment formula. We were staying at a bed and breakfast across the street from this property on a snowy weekend in January when we noticed that this historic mansion was being auctioned that same weekend. We had never purchased a property via auction before, and we were excited about the prospect of being able to own a charming little piece of history. We started thinking about how much we would be willing to pay for the property prior to attending the auction the following morning.

We went to the auction unprepared, without doing any prior inspections of the property, and without a clear idea of what we would do with the property if we won the auction. As with our other investments, we had intended to rent it. The property was different from the duplexes and single-family units we were used to. The historic mansion had been changed and expanded: it had a dentist's office on the first floor, a second floor with two rental units, and a top floor with one rental unit. It also had a parking lot in the back. It was much larger than our other investment properties and needed major renovation and work. Two of the rental properties were occupied by tenants but they were rented very cheaply and the tenants did not have a consistent history of paying. We somehow failed to appreciate these challenges when we put an offer on the property.

We were bidding against another individual and ended up paying $138,000 for it, which we thought was a great deal at the time. However, one of the things we didn't understand was that we also had to pay 10% commission to the auctioneer on top of that amount. We then spent considerable time, money, and effort trying to bring the property up to date so that we could rent it. We worked on the renovations ourselves, picking the paint and the fixtures, spending our weekends working there to save money. We remember going there with the contractor while we were pregnant with Natalie and painting the rental apartment on the top floor.

This property was an emotional buy for us and we wanted to do everything possible to make it work, even though we were having a very hard time even renting the commercial space on the first floor while simultaneously paying very high taxes and utility bills on a monthly basis. We had so many dreams about what we might do with the property, but it was bleeding money every month. After holding onto it for about eight months without successfully getting it rented, we decided it was best to let it go. We reached out to our real estate agent in Williamsport and asked him to put it up for sale. The market was pretty bad at the time, and we ended up losing about $20,000 on the property on top of all the other sunk cost. We sold it at a loss because we were desperate to stop the monthly expenses and stop the bleeding. We also wanted to continue investing in the types of properties that had worked for us the past.

LIFE-CHANGING EVENTS

All of us go through life-changing events that force us to make decisions. When you are in these situations, you tend to make decisions not only based on financial consideration—profit/loss on the property you are trying to sell—but other variables, including the effect of the situation you are in. These situations can include:

FAMILY GROWTH
You have a new addition to the family, but the current house is too small

SCHOOL DISTRICT
Your children are coming of age and you want to send your kids to a specific school district, so you need to move to that area and sell your current property

GETTING MARRIED
You may have a small apartment or house and need a starter home

BECOME UNEMPLOYED
When people become unemployed the burden of carrying a mortgage becomes a major concern and must be dealt with

CHANGE IN JOB/RELOCATION/MILITARY RELOCATION
For example, when we moved from New York to Virginia

PAYING TWO MORTGAGES
Changes in situation may put the seller in a position where he or she is paying two mortgages and needs to stop the losses as soon as possible

DEATH IN THE FAMILY
This is a tough and sad situation, but the family may need to sell their property

CONTINGENCY
Already purchased a new home contingent on sale of current home

BUILDING A NEW HOME
Bank financing on hold based on disposal of current property; for example, this was the case with our property on Boone Street

SELLER HAS BEEN TRANSFERRED
Transferred to another location and must sell in order to buy another house.

RETIRED AND MOVING

A lot of families want to relocate from their current area after they retire. Sometimes most of the property is paid off and they just need to move, and they're eager to get their investment back and make a profit, especially if they've held onto the property for thirty or forty years; some of these sellers will be willing to take a lower offer.

CHANGES IN THE AREA

If a base or manufacturing center is closing, this can motivate sellers in the area to divest their properties

RENTAL PROPERTIES/RENOVATION PROJECT GONE WRONG

We have bought a number of properties where the property is half-renovated, as if someone just got in over his head

In summary, a 'motivated seller' is a property owner who needs to sell the property fast and is willing to negotiate or take a price cut in order to sell the property. Not all motivated sellers are the same. We have learned that if you can understand the reason behind the motivation and work closely with your agent to structure a win-win deal, then you are one step closer to closing the deal.

If you have ever sold a property, then you may have an idea of what a motivated seller is. When we relocated from New York to Virginia, we owned a home in New York. CJ had a new job in Virginia and we were trying to purchase a home near his new company. We had a tough time buying a new house contingent on the sale of our home in New York. We needed to sell the house since we did not want to hold two mortgages, nor would a bank let us. We agreed to sell our home around $40K below market value because our home had been on the market for over six months. But the property had increased in value and we ended up with $60K in profits, which we used for a down payment on our new property in Virginia. At that time we were definitely motivated sellers in the job change/relocation category. I am sure the buyer believed they got a great deal, and we were extremely happy to sell that house to start our new life; in a situation like this, it was really a win-win for everyone even though we sold the property below market value.

Even in today's market, we continue to be able to find the deals that have helped us continue to grow. One of the interesting factors that has helped us grow our investments is that the deals come to us at times due to the relationships that we have built over time. Our real estate agents, our tenants, as well as our contractors, have all brought opportunities to us that had motivated sellers and have been great deals for us. In such scenarios, you can truly understand the need and at times you do not have to compete as you look to finalize the deal. In looking back at the past 3-5 years, we would say that at least three of the properties that we have purchased were brought to us and have allowed us to create a win-win situation as we continue to grow our real estate portfolio.

COUPLES' ACTION SUMMARY

If you need to look for good deals, you need to understand that life events play a major role in your buying strategy.

We believe that working with people to help them manage the changing events is not taking advantage of the situation, but rather helping people deal with the situation and move on with their lives.

As a couple, we look at properties and people's motives from different angles, and we base our understanding on our past experiences and individual understanding of human nature. We each have our own approach. As an example, CJ likes to ask short questions and listen to the answers, then make a decision on how to best make the next move. Like an engineer, he likes to think things through, analyze, and come up with a plan of action before moving forward. I like to develop a personal relationship early on and develop the conversation to build the trust needed to make the deal work. I can be quick on my feet, and my methods can achieve the same result as CJ's approach. We typically try to understand the communication style of the person we're working with and decide who's going to develop the relationship accordingly. We recommend that you identify how each one of you likes to do things and, based on each situation, determine who needs to lead. It could be a lot of fun it you realize this and test your approaches. You have nothing to lose—don't stress and just support each other in growing and learning the business.

NOTES

TASKS

CHAPTER FIVE

MONEY MATTERS: FINANCING AND PRICING STRATEGIES

One of the toughest decisions is to know when you're ready to invest, especially when it involves a significant amount of upfront funds. It's therefore very important to consider the following factors:

- Understand the true cost of a mortgage
- Weigh the pros and cons of financing versus cash deals
- Understand how long it will take to recover your initial investment
- Understand the potential additional costs that might arise
- Factor in vacancy when you're evaluating the mortgage option
- Understand your ROI: Jinan's secret formula for investment
- Understand how to price your house for refinancing if you plan to take a loan
- Understand the options for financing your property

UNDERSTANDING MORTGAGES

YOUR INCOME

Saving our income in order to invest was not easy. It involved a lot of sacrifices. We are lucky to have good jobs, but a lot of hard work went into earning our income, as we're sure is the same for most of you. You worked hard for your money; make sure you invest it wisely.

When we started talking about investments and property purchases, one of the hardest decisions we had to make was determining what we should pay for the property, how much mortgage we should take, how we could pay off the property in a short time period to minimize long-term risks. At the time we started investing we had a thirty-year mortgage and we certainly did not want to be in debt and at financial risk exposure with our investments for another thirty years. In our initial dealings with real estate agents, friends who invested, mortgage brokers, etc., everyone advised us to borrow as much as we could and build wealth using other people's money. We disagreed with that approach because we loathed being in debt and truly hated paying the high interest rates that apply to mortgages. In CJ's opinion, amortization schedules and the way that the mortgage industry is structured to give loans are truly in the interest of the banks and not the consumer. To better explain what we mean by that, consider this example: Our current mortgage on our house was around $540K, with a thirty-year mortgage and an interest rate of 5.85%. Without taxes and insurance, the monthly payment was $3,185.68. When your payments start, you would pay $553.18 a month in principle and $2,632.50 a month in interest. If you stay in the house for thirty years, you would pay $606,845.18 in interest on the property. At the end of thirty years, you would have to pay $1,146,845.18 for the property. The table below provides a summary of what we would pay if we stayed in our current property for thirty years.

LOAN SUMMARY

- Loan Interest Rate **5.85%**
- Original Loan Amount **$540,000**
- Monthly Principal & Interest **$3,185.68**
- Total Interest Paid **$606,845.18**
- Total of 360 Payments **$1,146,845.18**

When Jinan truly understood these numbers, she was shocked. Almost everyone says that you're not likely to stay in the same house for thirty years, and that you'll probably end up moving within two to five years. That's what we originally thought when we bought our house, so we did the math, and that was another surprise. After ten years, you would pay around $292K in interest on a $540K loan! That is almost 54% of the original loan value in interest alone over ten years, while you are only paying off about $90K of the original loan, which amounts to 16% of the original loan value. Below is a sample amortization schedule for the first ten years.

Year	Interest	Total Interest	Principal	Total Principal	Balance
1	$31,409.09	$31,409.09	$6,819.08	$6,819.08	$533,180.92
2	$30,999.30	$62,408.39	$7,228.87	$14,047.95	$525,952.05
3	$30,564.89	$92,973.28	$7,663.28	$21,711.23	$518,288.76
4	$30,104.37	$123,077.65	$8,123.80	$29,835.03	$510,164.96
5	$29,616.17	$152,693.82	$8,612.00	$38,447.03	$501,552.96
6	$29,098.64	$181,792.46	$9,129.53	$47,576.56	$492,423.43
7	$28,550.01	$210,342.47	$9,678.16	$57,254.72	$482,745.26
8	$27,968.41	$238,310.88	$10,259.77	$67,514.49	$472,485.50
9	$27,351.85	$265,662.73	$10,876.32	$78,390.81	$461,609.18
10	$26,698.25	$292,360.98	$11,529.92	$89,920.73	$450,079.25

Once you have the right tools, you'll see these numbers pretty easily. All you need to do is search the web for the keywords "Amortization Schedule Calculator" and you will find a lot of sample calculators with amortization schedules that you can use. The best site that we have used to review mortgage rates and utilize amortization calculators is BankRate.com.

This made it very clear for us that if were to invest for the long term we needed to find better options than financing. If we carried long-term mortgages, then most of our income after getting our investment properties renovated and rented would go to paying the interest on the loan. It's true that the value of the property is likely to increase over time, which helps build wealth—however, carrying a loan meant that our passive income would be paying for the interest. We had to come up with a way to reduce our debt.

UNDERSTANDING THE RULE OF FOUR

Traditional lenders will typically only allow you to have a maximum of four mortgages without additional requirements. In short, that means if you do not plan and budget right, once you get to your fourth property it will be more difficult to expand and get more mortgages. If you currently have a mortgage on your personal property, then you will only be able to get three additional mortgages. From our research and experience, we have found that some lenders will not issue more than four mortgages to an individual, but others may issue as many as ten mortgages to an individual. The number of mortgages will depend on a number of factors that include your credit score and percentage down. If you go with multiple vendors, you may be able to avoid some of these constraints. This all depends on the lenders and the risk you are willing to take. We tend to be very conservative investors and do not like to overextend ourselves. Another factor you need to consider is that the interest rates you get for your primary property (home) are typically much lower than the interest rates for an investment property. We truly do not recommend getting too many mortgages. We have opted to remain at three mortgages on all the properties that we own, and we now look for cash-based deals. In addition, we have changed our primary mortgage from thirty years to fifteen years, and we have the two investment properties with mortgages on them on a plan to be paid off in the next three years.

JINAN'S SECRET FORMULA FOR INVESTMENT

After buying a number of properties, Jinan asked CJ if he could come up with a formula or an approach that would allow us to quickly determine what we should offer for a given property we wanted to purchase. The formula needed to take into account how much rent we would need the property to generate if we were trying to pay it off or recoup our initial investment in five years. Finally, the formula needed to take into account a certain percentage of vacancy, as well as all costs associated with overhead (i.e. taxes, insurance, etc.) and a budget for repairs. In addition, the formula needed to be simple so that we could use it when making a quick offer on a property.

For the first couple of properties that we purchased, we had an elaborate spreadsheet that Jinan would use to compare properties before we made a decision. She remembers CJ staying up late in the hotel room while she was sleeping to have the numbers ready for us to review in the morning, an essential step before we could decide if we had any properties we wanted to revisit. It would take CJ hours to enter all the information to determine what we should offer for a property.

When we stated out in 2006, one day while we were having coffee and looking at printouts, Jinan told CJ that our current approach was too complicated. Looking back at what we'd bought as well as the current analysis we were reviewing, she asked, "If we say we need to make $1,000 in rent per month for every $60K we invest, would that work? If fully rented, that would be $12K per year; in six-eight years that gives you $72K in income (taking expenses into account), and if we put some money down and focus we should get our entire investment back in six to eight years. It would be up to us to figure out how to pay down the mortgage and down payment." Over the years, we have focused and worked hard to apply the formula in our negotiations for properties. If the formula does not work or it is not close, we walk away.

Summary of the initial analysis that we use to drive our property evaluation:

- Every $60,000 invested needs to generate $1,000 in monthly income
- Every $30,000 invested needs to generate $500 in monthly income
- Every $15,000 invested needs to generate $250 in monthly investment

As a general guideline based on the formula, the property would pay for itself within six-eight years from the gross rental income it generates, assuming that the value of the property stays the same and takes into account expenses. For example, when we invest $60,000 for a new rental property, we expect it to generate $1,000 a month in rent or $12,000 in gross income annually. Today we also factor that 30-40 percent of the gross income is put aside to support expenses and investment growth.

When looking at properties, we can now use the above table as a simple guideline and make a quick decision about whether the price makes sense. Of course, it's important to understand the rental potential of the property, and we apply a conservative approach in estimating the monthly rent after consulting our property management company.

Our simple formula can be simplified mathematically so that every $1 invested needs to generate $.0166 in monthly rental income.

In order to determine whether to purchase a property, we can apply our formula to see how much rent is needed in order for us to meet our formula objectives:

Minimum rent needed = (Purchase price + renovation cost) x (0.0166)

We have been lucky to have been able to find properties that fall within our formula. Over the years, depending on the area and investment locale, we have worked with many folks that have read our first book to help them make decisions on understanding their local market and tailor their investment strategies to achieve their goals.

Using this formula as a baseline will force you to look at properties from a different perspective. As an example, a property that sells for $300K needs to provide a monthly rental income of close to $5K per month—if not, what other factors and/or investment options do you have in order to grow your portfolio while still meeting your investment objectives?

In Chapter Fifteen of this book we provide an approach to modifying or tailoring our formula to fit your needs, risks, and the markets you are researching that aren't covered by our approach.

COUPLES' ACTION SUMMARY

As a couple, we have always looked at our finances and spending on a monthly basis while taking into account where we would like to be in the future. We have always considered our savings as well as investment accounts. In order to develop this understanding, you need to be organized and have access to your different accounts both online and on paper. It is also important that you make the time to communicate to your partner your current financial position so that both of you can make educated spending and saving decisions.

We have an open policy about sharing information regarding our financial status with each other. We have shared bank accounts, to which both of us have full access and control. Our paychecks are automatically deposited into these accounts. We were surprised when we would talk to different working couples where each spouse has a separate bank account and each one pays for their bills, or they have shared bills and they can spend the rest of the money any way they wish since they earned their share of the paycheck. We do not believe in this separation, but believe in working hard as a couple and developing the trust needed between us to succeed.

continued

COUPLES' ACTION SUMMARY

For us, it doesn't matter who makes more money or who earns what. We both believe in working hard and dealing with our expenses together. Sharing our financial standing with each other has helped us develop the understanding that we are one and that financial decisions need to be taken as a team.

As you start investing, work as a team to make sure that you develop and follow a profitability formula to narrow down your decision.

- Look at the numbers and make sure they make sense
- Consider other important factors to make sure your property will bring you good return on investment
- ☺ Be positive when looking at your current investments and put in place steps to help you move forward

Most importantly, make sure it is always a joint decision—never buy a property without the mutual agreed decision of both partners.

NOTES

NOTES

TASKS

CHAPTER SIX

NEGOTIATION STRATEGIES

Negotiation is key for a successful investor—without negotiation skills and a willingness to engage in negotiations, you will not succeed as an investor

- ☺ Negotiations help you achieve your planned objectives
- An educated buyer is key to winning a negotiation
- Understanding the seller's motivation to sell is key to putting the best offer forward
- Negotiation is an art and should not be rushed; take time to plan and execute your strategy
- Everything is negotiable, just ask
- Be willing to walk away if necessary
- ✭ You will make mistakes, but you need to learn from them
- No one is forcing you to buy—you are in the driver's seat, and you can always walk away

THE IMPORTANCE OF UNDERSTANDING NEGOTIATIONS

ALWAYS NEGOTIATE!

If you don't negotiate, you're leaving money on the table. Always be ready to negotiate. Put yourself in the other party's shoes and understand where they're coming from. You'll be surprised what you can get away with.

In order to be successful in business, you have to be able to negotiate. Negotiation is not only about the closing price on a given property but truly about how you run and conduct the different aspects of your business. If you are not able to understand your position, negotiate your position, and achieve a favorable position, you will not be successful in your efforts. By expanding the pie when negotiating, you can make sure that everyone gets a fair share in a deal.

People skills, as well as communication skills, will need to become a critical part of your skill set. When we were starting out, we had to develop these skills. One thing that helped us get started was that we both interact with people as part of our day jobs. However, dealing with our first couple of transactions, we still felt like fish out of water. As we worked through them, we developed confidence when dealing with situations that we weren't typically comfortable with. We had to learn that we truly are in control of the situation; that helped us gain the confidence to take the tough positions we needed to take in order to be successful. This took us years to learn and we still deal with new situations on a regular basis that force us to go back to the basics and make sure we are making the right business decisions for our investments.

Based on our experiences and interactions, we have the following recommendations about what you take into account when negotiating the deal. Most of the recommendations mentioned in this chapter are used in our daily business interactions.

PLANNING: UNDERSTANDING THE SELLER'S MOTIVATION AND POSITION

As we have mentioned earlier, people sell for many reasons. By understanding why someone is selling the property, you will be better positioned to tailor your offer. We believe that this is an important factor.

- Understand the property's history prior to making an offer.
- Understand the reason why the property is listed for sale.
- Is the seller under any time constraint? How long has the property been for sale? If the seller is in a rush to sell the property and the property has been on the market for

a long time, the seller may be willing to accept a lower offer on the property.

- Has the owner tried to sell the property before? You will be surprised how many times the owners of some properties have tried to sell and then taken them off the market.
- Does the property have a current mortgage on it, and what is the current mortgage? Understanding the mortgage may give you the bottom line a seller might be willing to settle for depending on the situation.
- How long has the seller owned the property and what was the purchase price?
- Play a role in the negotiation process—you need to have a poker face and always focus on the negative things you see in the property you're buying to reduce the price (similar to when you're buying a car—especially a used one!).
- No one is forcing the seller to sell you the house with the issues found; they can fix it or reduce the price to allow you to deal with it.
- Always let everyone know you are a serious investor, but you are ready to walk away from the deal if it does not make financial sense for you.

We never offer asking price or even market price for any of the properties that we purchase. We know the bargains come when the seller is motivated; if the seller is not motivated, we probably will not get the deal we are looking for. You have to be willing to walk away from a deal. If the seller is motivated and understands that you are willing to walk away, they will negotiate on the price. After we do our research and establish value, we typically offer 25-30% below our own estimate or the asking price as a first price to see if we have room for negotiation. Most of the time we receive a counteroffer and then we can start working. If we do not get a counteroffer we tend to move on to the next property.

There are many ways you can find out more about the property. When we started working, we found the people providing us with the least useful information were our own real estate agents. We still do not fully understand why, but it may have to do with a real estate agent working as a seller agent even when they are not the listing agent on the property. A seller agent may not have your best interests in mind and may share information about the buyer with the seller that will affect the sale or the price. Most real estate agents wanted us to avoid in-depth discussions with the owners or tenants of properties that we walked through. In our approach, we need to get more information about the property in order to tailor the offer. Early on, when we started investing, we realized that as a couple walking through the property we had an advantage: one of us would distract the real estate agent while the other talked to the owner or tenants and got valuable information about the property. This is no longer an issue, since the property managers we work with are real estate agents and act as a buyer's agent; they work with us to provide us as much information as we need to understand the deal and ensure it makes financial sense to us. We believe in working with real estate agents since they are the experts in their fields, but we only work with them as buyer's agents.

In addition, we found that the Internet is full of resources to help us research properties we are interested in. Sites such as Zillow.com provide a wealth of information on a property. These sites typically provide information like:

- Current estimate/property appraisal value
- Property public records
- Property tax information
- Property description
- Ability to look at areas and look at sale price of adjacent properties. This will give you an idea of the market and potential value of the property if fixed up.

Another thing we typically try to look at is the tax records related to the property. Your property manager or real estate agent can provide you with a copy of the property tax records. In order to understand the seller's motivation, you can look at the following factors:

- Is the house vacant? If so, how long has it been vacant?
- Is the property maintained? (Is the grass cut, etc.)
- How many people are living in the house?
- ? What information is available about the family currently living there?
- How long has the house been listed?
- $ How many times has the price been reduced recently, and by how much?

In the end, it is your decision—make sure you are making informed decisions and not rushing into any investments.

SEPARATE EMOTIONAL ATTACHMENTS FROM INVESTMENT DECISIONS

One of the hardest things for us was learning to detach ourselves emotionally from our investment decisions. All of us come from different cultures, traditions, and ways of doing things. Our background, our values, and our dreams will sometimes mask and confuse the decision-making process when dealing with a difficult situation.

As an example, we went into the hunt for our sixth property feeling good. We had been successful in our last three purchases and we were looking forward to the next one. As we were looking at the options, one property caught CJ's attention. It was a three-story duplex in the historic district with huge potential for curb appeal, as it was next to a river. It was priced very well and our property manager informed us that the owner was very motivated to sell. On paper everything looked perfect and CJ just fell in love with the property as a whole. When we did our walk-through, we realized the place needed a tremendous amount of work. The roof was leaking, it had electric wiring issues, and the previous owner had tried to convert the duplex into a single unit with a huge open-plan kitchen. We were not sure if the property had any structural damage, but it had some walls that were not very straight. When we looked at the renovation costs, they would have been tremendous.

Despite all its issues and the potential pitfalls of this property, CJ was emotionally attached to the building and could not see all the risks involved in the purchase. In addition, we were informed that a number of people were giving offers on the property and we did not have a lot of time to make the decision. This was a tough decision point for us—Jinan did not want to disappoint CJ, knowing how much he liked the property, but was very concerned about the financial pitfalls and risks associated with this property. In order to make the decision, we had to step back and look at why we invest: revisit our long-term goals, how much money we had, and the true budget for making this a successful property. When we looked at the numbers associated with renovation from a business point of view, we had to walk away, and we did. We did not make an offer on the building. It was bought by another investor for a bargain price—at least, that was what CJ thought at the time. On an interesting note, three years later, we were driving through the same neighborhood to look at another property and we passed by this building; we saw scaffolds on the outside and it looked like construction was still ongoing. As we talked about the building, we both smiled; we were so thankful that we'd walked away and knew we'd made the right decision.

There have also been times when Jinan was emotionally attached to property, but it is no longer an issue; today we just look at properties from a business perspective and keep emotions out of it. We have no problem walking away from a property, regardless of how much time was invested into looking into it. If it doesn't make financial sense for us, we make the tough decision and move on.

NATALIE'S RULES OF NEGOTIATION: LESSONS LEARNED FROM OUR DAUGHTER

If you have kids, you know that they have a miraculous way of somehow always getting what they want. In looking at the power of negotiation, it always amazes us to see Natalie in action.

For example, when her grandma and grandpa are visiting, she knows she can get pretty much anything she wants. If she asks for something from Grandpa and he doesn't give her what she wants, she'll go to Grandma and ask again, and she'll usually get what she's after. This also works in reverse. It's amazing how she understands the roles of different players in our family and she can assess the pull she has with each one of us. Even at her young age, she understands that by using a different approach with each person, she can greatly improve her chances of getting what she wants. For example, she knows that by being very affectionate and giving her dad a kiss on the cheek, she's pretty much guaranteed to get it. One of the tricks that she tries on Jinan is to say, "Oh, Mommy! Your dress is so beautiful!" If nothing else, she always gets a smile and my attention with that.

Another thing we've learned from her: Rather than getting into an argument when you can't get what you want, use negotiation to compromise and at least get some of your demands met. For example, when it's time for Natalie to sleep and she wants to watch TV, she knows that by asking gently to watch five or ten more minutes of TV, we'll usually say yes. As a master negotiator, she always starts by asking for more than what she thinks she'll get away with. This also works well for her when she's eating her favorite chocolate ice cream. She always starts by asking, "Mommy, can I eat the whole thing?" Jinan will say, "No, you can only have three spoons." She'll then come back and say, "How about five?" and she often gets away with that.

The other thing that we find truly amazing about Natalie is her ability to manipulate the situation to her advantage. For example, even though she hates taking her afternoon nap, she has learned that instead of crying and fighting it like she used to, she's better off using it as a bait-and-switch tool to get something she wants from me. For example, she'll say, "If I sleep for half an hour, will you promise to take me to the mall/swimming pool/park when I wake up?" Of course, the answer is almost always yes. She still hates her afternoon nap, but at least now she's figured out a creative way to get something she likes out of it.

Lessons learned from Natalie that can be used during negotiations:

- Understand who's the decision-maker
- When you are unhappy with the decision, make that clear (do not cry) and walk away, and try to use the situation to your advantage whenever possible
- If you dealing with multiple decision-makers, and you do not get the answer that you want to hear from the first person, just ask the other person and make them negotiate
- ☺ Always smile and show them how much you enjoy working with them

THE TWENTY-FOUR-HOUR RULE

One of our simple rules is that regardless of how good the deal looks, or whatever reason someone gives us as to why we need to sign now, our position has always been that we do not sign anything unless we sleep on it for one day. This position has stressed a lot of people, especially those trying to sell us something or push us to make decisions. However, it has truly helped us refine our decisions and I believe it is one of the major factors that had allowed us to walk away from bad deals. If the deal can't wait twenty-four hours, it is not for us. This position also helps us walk away from the table and discuss our options before we finalize our decision or offer.

This is a very important position to us, and if we are in what is perceived as a pressure sale situation, we communicate this position early on in the conversation and make sure the other party is aware of our approach. When the time for the pressure sale comes—and we have learned to look for it—all we have to do is remind the other party of our approach and politely inform them that we will provide them our answer soon, but that we need at least twenty-four hours.

I'm sure we've all been through a pressure sale. One that comes to mind immediately is when we went to the Bahamas for our anniversary and we decided to attend one of the time-share resort presentations. After the presentation and tour of the resort property, we went into the salesperson's office, where we stayed for over two hours as she tried to use pressure-sale tactics to convince us that we needed to buy the time-share and that she could only hold the special price for that day. But we had already been burned by other pressure sales and learned from that experience. We stuck to the twenty-four-hour rule without any regrets.

EVERY DOLLAR COUNTS

When you spend money in an unmanaged way, you can be spending hundreds or thousands of dollars without realizing how much you are spending. Every day, you are faced with different decisions that affect your spending. As the number of your properties grows and as your contacts grow, the decisions you have to make on a regular basis grow as well. Whether you are making a decision to spend $100 or $1,000, your decisions affect your bottom line. When negotiating a deal, people tend to push you to spend by saying that the price they want is only $1,000 more than you wanted to spend, or something along these lines. CJ's position is always to take a step back and not to rush. He always explains that we will have to make at least one hundred unplanned decisions every year on various things. If the cost of each unplanned decision is $1,000, you just spent $100,000 without even realizing that you spent it. These unplanned decisions come at random times and they are not typically tied together. If different people have the authority to make these decisions and they are not communicating, the problem is compounded. We always talk about spending with each other no matter how small or stupid it is; we use each other as support and talk through it. Even if one of us knows what the decision is, and can make the decision easily, we talk it through and explain why we should spend the money and what we need to spend it on.

Being frugal and taking a step back to truly understand and analyze a spending decision is smart business sense if you want to be successful and profitable in the long term. If someone thinks you're cheap for needing time to finalize your decision, you may want to re-evaluate your relationship with them and understand in whose best interest they are working.

LISTENING AND CONTINUOUS COMMUNICATIONS AND FOLLOW-UP: BEING PROACTIVE

In order to win in a negotiation, you need to understand the position of the other side. A lot of times, when we buy a property, that purchase is based on understanding the seller's motivation:

being able to put a proposal on the table that addresses the seller's needs and to tailor our offer to those needs. We believe that when you propose a deal, no one is forcing the other side to accept; the other side might have their own pressures and reasons for wanting to make the deal happen, and if you understand these pressures you can position the deal to work best for you. If you are dealing with bank-owned properties, you need to understand the bank's motivating factors to sell. If you are dealing with sellers, you need to understand why the property is listed for sale and use those factors to compose the structure of your deal. You always need to be willing to think outside the box in order to finalize the deal.

One of CJ's friends was trying to purchase a property in Ashburn, Virginia; he had placed a couple of bids on a number of houses, he was submitting offer prices, but none of the offers he put through came in. He was getting frustrated: his wife was expecting a baby, his lease was about to expire in a couple of months, and he truly wanted to get a home for his family. It was going to be his first true home. It was truly a seller's market. One day over lunch he expressed his frustration to CJ. CJ's advice was get to know the seller—it can be little things that make a deal come through.

CJ's friend kept looking and after a couple of weeks, he told me that he'd found the perfect house but was locked in a bidding war between them and another couple. CJ asked if he'd talked to the owner and his friend informed us that he had—the owner was confused about whose offer to accept. The owner was about to move but had to take care of a couple things: his washer and dryer (which couldn't be moved) and some bedroom furniture. The owner was primarily focused on what to do with the leftover furniture, as well as other items that he couldn't take with him. CJ recommended that his friend call back the owner and let him know that he would offer an additional $3K to take care of the items that the owner couldn't move. He told his friend to modify his offer so that he was bidding near the top and to ensure that he talked to the owner, told him about his situation, and created a relationship, letting the owner he was willing to work through any issues to ensure the deal went through. CJ's friend followed this advice and he got the house.

OTHER NEGOTIATION TIPS

GENERAL NEGOTIATION CONSIDERATION	DETAILS
LOOSE LIPS SINK SHIPS (KNOW THE IMPORTANCE OF SILENCE)	Only share information that needs to be shared. You will never know how people interpret information and how they react to it. The same way you try to understand the seller's motivation, someone might be doing the same for you, i.e. trying to understand your budget, your motivation to buy, how much you could potentially spend, etc.
YOU GET MORE FLIES WITH HONEY—ANGER AND YELLING DO NOT RESOLVE ISSUES	Always deal with issues from a business point of view. In addition, remember you are doing this for the fun of investing. You will be in situations in which you are furious; our recommendation is to take a deep breath and deal with the situation in a calm and easy manner. Sometimes people just make mistakes and don't realize it. By talking through the issues, you truly get a lot further than if you lose your temper.
DON'T UNDERESTIMATE THE STRENGTH OF RELATIONSHIPS, RESEARCH AND NETWORKING	Reaching out to your connections to ask questions and leaning on experts for advice will help you in your negotiations.

GENERAL NEGOTIATION CONSIDERATION	DETAILS
EMPLOY RESPECT AND TRUTHFULNESS (AIM FOR THE WIN/WIN)	You live by reputation; people will deal with you based on how you deal with them. We always deal with people in the way we would like others to deal with us.
PATIENCE AND ETHICS ARE VIRTUES	Typically you will end up working with like-minded people. If you are working with folks who do not have the same ethics that you do, find someone who does.
EVERYTHING IS NEGOTIABLE, YOU JUST NEED TO ASK	At times people tell us that we should not ask for certain things, because things are done one way in this industry, or that something is impossible and you should not even try for it. There may be situations when you are not sure if you can negotiate a point. Keep in mind that you are doing this for the future of your family. If you think you can negotiate something, all you need to do is ask—you have nothing to lose if you are willing to walk away.
FRAMING AND EXPANDING THE PIE	If we learned one critical thing from our MBA classes, it is that how you present the issue will make a huge difference in the end. Once you understand the position that you would like to achieve, always think on how best to present it such that it makes sense or is attractive to the other party.
KEEP IT SIMPLE AND ASK LEADING QUESTIONS	When you are not sure of the exact position of the other party, try to ask the right questions to get the answers you need before you make a decision.

COUPLES' ACTION SUMMARY

Being a couple has several advantages in negotiation. For example, you can play bad cop/good cop. Leverage each other's strengths when negotiating a deal. Take the time to discuss the offer, listen to each other's thoughts, and put in place a strategy to make the deal happen.

It is important as a couple that you have an understanding of and agreement on your objectives. Many times, we thought that we were in agreement, and the situation changed, making it necessary for us to discuss further before making a decision. I can say that we have been caught off guard and that we have made mistakes. We have always tried to learn from our mistakes when we make the next deal. During one of our conversations with our book publisher, we mentioned that our view is that "learning from your mistakes makes you stronger;" his answer to us was, "I am fine the way I am—I'd much rather not get stronger and not to have to deal with mistakes." We all started laughing.

The most important thing is that if you as a couple are caught off guard, and you realize a mistake has been made during a negotiation, be willing to take corrective actions and be willing to walk away, especially if you are not legally bound. You need to always remember that this is a business transaction, and at times you need to make uncomfortable decisions in order to protect your current investments and ensure you can continue to invest for your future.

When faced with a situation in which one of you decides you need more time to make a decision, we strongly recommend that you make time to discuss. As an example:

COUPLES' ACTION SUMMARY

- You can use the need to discuss the situation with your spouse as an excuse for not making a decision on the spot
- Understand that when you're together in the same room, the pressure to make a decision right there and then is much higher. You need to be ready to share your twenty-four-hour rule about making any decision and ask for more time.
- Develop a secret code of communication between you so that when you're in a situation where you're asked to make a decision on the spot, you can ask for more time to finalize your decision.

NOTES

TASKS

- [ ]
- [ ]
- [ ]
- [ ]
- [ ]
- [ ]
- [ ]
- [ ]
- [ ]

G2

CHAPTER SEVEN

BUILDING YOUR EXTERNAL SUPPORT TEAM

In order to be successful, you need to build a network of connections that you can trust and who can help you succeed in accomplishing your goals

- In our opinion, the most important external relationship is finding the right property management company to work with you
- You can work with different property management companies in different geographical areas
- Our second most important team was our tax accountant and insurance agents
- When we started out, our third most important team was our lenders
- A strong relationship with a local attorney who can help close deals, and a person who can support you in any legal issues, is also very important
- Having a support team that can answer questions in a timely manner will go a long way toward helping you succeed in your investment efforts
- You need to ensure that you work with experienced people who understand the needs of an investor
- Have fun building your relationships and make new friends
- We like to support the local economy and use local resources

MAKE NEW FRIENDS

Over the years we have met so many new people whom we have gotten to know both on the personal and business levels. These relationships have truly helped us succeed in our efforts and have added a lot of sugar and spice to our lives. Be ready to meet new people and develop new relationships as you explore your business opportunities.

YOUR EXTERNAL SUPPORT

When we first started investing we truly had no support network. We had purchased our land in West Virginia as our first investment, but we did not have a full understanding of how financing works. During the process of purchasing our land in West Virginia, we got introduced to a VP at a local bank who was responsible for assisting us in the financing process. During the qualifying process we got to know her very well. She was extremely helpful; she worked with us to ensure everything went smoothly and explained to us how the process works. When we decided to pursue our investment strategy I called her and explained to her what we were trying to do in terms of investment, and she helped us by providing us with a number of options, as well as qualifying us in the process of refinancing our home, paying off the land we had purchased, and providing funds for the purchase of our first rental property. It was very interesting that the VP strongly recommended to us not to extend ourselves too much, to be conservative in our financial endeavors and to take calculated risks. We had a lot of credit and we could have extended ourselves much more, but we followed her advice to be conservative. This advice paid off when the housing market crashed—due to her conservative advice, it did not truly affect us. The VP has introduced us to her internal network at the bank and it has been a great relationship for us. We have found that working with smaller regional banks with the small business mentality is much better than working with larger banks.

Our first purchase was made through working with a real estate agent. We just called the real estate office in Cumberland and they assigned us a real estate agent. We did not truly ask any questions about the qualifications of the real estate agent. We were assigned a new real estate agent—if I remember correctly, we were actually one of the first clients she sold a property with. She had great energy and an amazing personality, and was trying her hardest to help us, but as we worked with her to look at properties, it was obvious that she was not an experienced real estate agent and she always had to reference back to the broker to answer our questions. We had already signed some exclusive paperwork and we decided to continue working with her since we did not know any better at the time. We took proactive measures to understand the process, learning how to look at local listings and then coordinating with her. One thing I remember vividly was her insistence that we needed to sign paperwork indicating that she was a seller's agent and not a buyer's agent. Today, our property managers are our real estate agents and we always work with them as buyer's agents, not as seller's agents.

We also found that it does not cost you any more money for a real estate agent to be a buyer's agent instead of a seller's agent. When we draft the agreement, the commission paid to the agent is the spilt commission from the purchase of the property that we would have had to pay anyway. It took us time to understand the differences, and while we still do not fully understand it, we recommend that you try to work with your agent as a buyer's agent. Below is a high-level definition of each; the definitions are based on the state of Maryland definitions as we understand them, but they may be different across states.

SELLER'S AGENT

A seller's agent works for the real estate company that lists and markets the property for the sellers and exclusively represents the sellers. That means that the seller's agent may assist the buyer in purchasing the property, but his or her duty or loyalty is only to the seller.

COOPERATING AGENT

A cooperating agent works for a real estate company different from the company for which the seller's agent works. The cooperating agent can assist a buyer in purchasing a property, but his or her duty or loyalty is only to the sellers.

BUYER'S AGENT (BY WRITTEN AGREEMENT)

A buyer may enter into a written contract with a real estate agent which provides that the agent will represent the buyer in locating a property to buy. The agent is then known as the buyer's agent. That agent assists the buyer in evaluating properties and preparing offers, and negotiates in the best interests of the buyer. The agent's fee is paid according to the written agreement between the agent and the buyer. If you as a buyer wish to have an agent represent you, you must enter into a written buyer agency agreement before a contract offer can be prepared.

Working with good real estate agents has helped us get where we needed to go. We recommend discussing the different roles with them and making the decision that's right for you. Real estate agents understand the ins and outs of the local markets they work in; they understand the values of the different neighborhoods and can help steer you in the right direction to find the property that you need. Still, always remember that whether or not to buy is your decision. We truly believe in the value of real estate agents and do not recommend buying a property without working with an agent. Still, in the end, you need to make an educated decision on whether to move forward based on your investment strategies.

WORKING WITH PROPERTY MANAGERS: YOUR MOST IMPORTANT RELATIONSHIP

When we started thinking about investments and we wanted to focus our investment for the long term, one of our main challenges was figuring out how to manage the properties. Some of our issues and concerns included:

- How will we find and screen tenants?
- What is the best way to fix the properties and get them rented?

- How will we manage our properties while still working our day jobs?
- Do we want tenants calling us all day for different needs?
- Do we need to get a second cell phone/land line just for the tenants?
- $ How do we deal with collection issues if tenants don't pay on time?

These are just a few of the questions we were asking ourselves when we were thinking about how to manage our properties. When we looked at investment areas that made financial sense, none of the areas were local. Most of the books that we'd read talked about how to screen and manage tenants, how to repair a property if something broke, the need to build relationships with contractors, etc. Few or none of the books talked about property managers. Some books mentioned the value of property managers, but none of the books that we read focused on making property managers a key success factor in the investment strategy. One of the reasons that people invest in mutual funds or stocks is that most people use fund managers or stockbrokers to manage their investments. When we invest in 401(k) we depend on other people to manage our money, and they all take a fee one way or another for those management services. The majority of those who invest in mutual funds or 401(k) will never meet the people or fund managers who earn a fee based on our funds, and most of us are just numbers in a large portfolio. Interestingly, fund managers typically get a bonus regardless of the performance of the fund.

A property manager is very similar to a fund manager. The important difference is that you have a close relationship with your property manager; they get to know you personally and you get to know them. You can build a relationship of trust that works for both of you, and when your property is making money for you, they are making money as well. If they are not making money for you, they are not making money from your properties and it's a missed opportunity for additional income. Working with a property manager creates a win-win relationship that benefits both parties.

It took us years to fully comprehend this. When we first started investing, we had decided to separate the role of the property manager from the role of the real estate agent. We tried to build relationships with both the property manager and the real estate agents. We soon came to realize that the real estate agent's interest is a bit different from the property manager's. In addition, we found out that most property managers are also real estate agents.

In the beginning, we would find a property by working with a real estate agent, then contact the property manager and ask him or her to look at the property prior to purchase. The real estate agent and the property manager would look at the same property from two different angles. As an example, at one of the properties that we were looking at, the real estate agent and the property manager got into an argument over differences of opinion. We had been looking for a couple of months for the next investment property and we had narrowed down our options to two potential properties. The real estate agent had spent time and effort getting the listings to us for review, analyzing the properties, and sending us pictures, and had, when we visited the area on two occasions, spent around ten hours helping us narrow down our options.

We had made it clear that the final decision to purchase the property depended on its rental potential, the area where it was located and the renovation cost of the property. The real estate agent and the property manager argued over the rental potential of the property and the renovation estimates to get it ready for rental. The property manager brought the layout of the house to our attention, along with other factors that were important for estimating the renovation cost. On that particular property, getting to the main bathroom required going through the kitchen. Once we looked at it more closely, we realized the oddness of the property's layout. It also seemed that the roof had some problems we were advised to look at closely. The property manager was able to point out areas in the house that the seller had tried to hide, such as watermarks. In addition, when we stepped away from the house and took a look at the roof from far away, it appeared to be sagging. The property manager recommended that we make a closer inspection of the issues and consider them in the asking price of the property. The property was being sold "as is."

In the end, we had to agree with the property manager. In taking a $300 hit to get the property fully inspected, we uncovered multiple issues that would have cost us a lot of money in the renovation process. The major lesson learned from this experience was that a property manager looks at a property which is being purchased with a vested interest in ensuring that property is rentable, since this is how the property manager makes money.

Some of the advantages of working with a property manager include:

- A property manager will be the first line of defense between you and any issues associated with managing your property. Property managers are experts at dealing with the day-to-day operations of your properties.
- Property managers can help with management of your cash flow, if necessary.
- Property managers generally have established relationships with good contractors even before you come into the picture, and they can help you work with contractors to pay for repairs over a number of months, using the monthly income you're earning from your property.
- Property managers deal directly with tenants in the areas of maintenance, repairs, rent rates, and rent collection.

- Property managers understand the local city and state laws and they can help ensure you get proper inspections and adhere to local laws, as well as supporting you if you have to manage tenants who fail to pay the rent.
- They can act as your local agent. Many cities will not allow people without a local agent to manage a property. This is true in both Cumberland and Williamsport; our property managers act as our agents.
- Property managers likely know the local inspectors and can coordinate inspections for you.
- A property manager makes money when you make money and builds relationships with the local community by working with you.

We have worked with several different property managers, and each office works differently in terms of fees and contract terms. Contract terms to take into account when dealing with a property manager include:

- Placement fee: A placement fee is a fee taken when a new tenant is placed on the property. Some property managers will take the first month's rent as their placement fee and others have a set fee per placement.
- Percentage of monthly income: Around 10% per month of your income from a rental property will go to the property manager—that is the current average.
- Reserve amount: The amount of money that a property manager will leave in reserve from the rent in order to ensure they can quickly address emergency repairs.
- The amount of money they have the authority to spend prior to reaching out to you.
- Statement of responsibilities.

It is also important to choose the right management company. In one of the areas where we invest, we had to go through three property managers until we found the right one. Some of our challenges in dealing with property managers included:

- Competition in rentals: Some property manager work for a real estate firm that has their own rental investment properties, and we have found that at times this creates a situation where there is a conflict of interest. When demand for rentals was low, property managers sometimes filled rentals owned by the real estate company prior to filling our vacancies. We no longer work with the property management company that did this.
- Engaging the services of friends or family to perform contracting or maintenance jobs on our properties even if they are not as price competitive as other local bidders.

Make sure you are getting multiple bids for the work being proposed. Some of our recommendations for choosing a property management company follow:

- Work with small companies that are dedicated
- Understand how many properties are typically managed by the propertymanager
- Work with a property management company that can also represent you as a real estate agent
- Work with a property management company that has been in the area for a long time
- Work with a property management company that has established relationships with contractors, inspectors, maintenance crews, and local authorities in case you need to deal with evacuating a tenant

In the process of writing this book, during a meeting with one of the property manages, we mentioned how much we value and appreciate working with property management companies. He smiled and told us that not all owners are like us. Our approach to property investment, he said, is different than other owners, and he really enjoys working with us. He indicated that one of the things that is important to his property management company is that they treat every property as if it were their own. He said he enjoys working with us so much that sometimes on weekends he just drives around our properties, trims the trees, ensures our sidewalks are clean and, for vacant properties waiting to be rented, he plants flowers to improve the curb appeal. Hearing this from him was touching and strengthened our belief in the value of property managers; our property managers have truly been our mentors throughout our investment journey. It is all about establishing the right relationship and trust; if done right, it can be very rewarding.

MISTAKES OFTEN MADE BY THE UNINFORMED: NOTES AND THOUGHTS FROM ONE OF OUR PROPERTY MANAGERS, MR. VIRGIL TWIGG, CUMBERLAND, MD

We asked Virgil if he had some thoughts about real estate investment that he'd be willing to add to our book so that all our readers could benefit from his experience. In response, he provided us with the write-up in this section.

There are probably as many reasons people choose to invest in real estate as there are houses to buy. Long before Cumberland became a "hot bed" for investors, I told anyone who would listen, "If it doesn't work out on paper, it won't work." The trick, of course, is knowing what to put on the paper.

In thirty-seven years of working with investors I have, too many times, had to sit down with owners and ask them if, prior to purchasing a property, they had given any thought to income and expenses.

Almost every one of us has been bombarded by the TV infomercials advertising a scheme through which you can "buy with no money down" and retire.

In recent years, I have seen novice investors come to Cumberland from the Metropolitan areas of Washington, Baltimore, Northern Virginia, California, and New York. They do not realize that everything is relative. Yes, $50,000.00 may sound like a real bargain to someone with an annual family income of $300,000.00 from Washington, where a two-bedroom apartment rents for $1,200.00 per month. In Cumberland, only an unusually nice home rents for $1,200.00 per month. In fact I am not sure there is one being rented for that much. Novice investors can hardly wait to "jump in."

Let's explore for a minute some of the nuances of an investment property that might make a real difference.

1. Location: We have all heard that old axiom: "The three most important things about a property are location, location, location." That is entirely true, but that doesn't mean that the worst location in town couldn't be a very good place to purchase an investment property. As a matter of fact, the worst part of any town is probably 95% rental units. You just have to buy at the right price.

2. Units: I mention this just so I'm sure we're on the same page. One building with three apartments is a three-unit dwelling. A single-family home is a one-unit dwelling. That's really elementary, but there are some significant financial ramifications of choosing one unit count over another. As an example, a single-family dwelling that becomes vacant and can't be rented for two months has just lost 16% of its annual income. The same scenario for one two-month vacancy in a two-unit dwelling means the dwelling has lost only 8% of its annual income.

3. The location of the building is not the only location worth looking at. The location of a unit in a building is also important. Just ask the tenant on the second floor about that bass music coming up through the floor from the tenant below. Then ask the tenant down below about the tenant above, who vacuums his floor for an hour every morning at 6:00 a.m. To illustrate this point, we once had to evict a very good HUD tenant who resided on the first level of a two-unit building, after she insisted on calling the police because the tenant above her refused to refrain from walking across the floor of her apartment at 6:00 p.m.—the downstairs tenant's bedtime. The police could not stop her from calling them. She had lived in that unit for four years and peacefully coexisted with two other tenants above her. We really suspected this whole situation arose because of pets—each tenant had a pet dog. (The lower-level tenant had never had to contend with someone else in her building with a pet.) We determined it was in the owners' best interest to find a replacement tenant. Problems cause vacancies. Vacancies cause problems. Prepare yourself.

Some other conditions than worsen a property's appeal include but are certainly not limited to long access steps, either from the street to the dwelling or for access to upper levels. (Stairways need to be cleared of snow and ice. Tenants don't want to do it and if the owner contracts for it, the cash flow for that unit is adversely affected.)

4. Site size: This covers the location of the dwelling on the site and the yards—front, side, and back. This might sound trivial, but if the property in which you are interested has two three-bedroom units with no place for children to play, your units may need some other amenity or amenities to stand toe-to-toe to your competition.

5. Parking can make a difference. Normally, an alley with access to a rear yard or some type of onsite parking has a positive influence on tenants and can make your investment easier to rent, and therefore make it easier for you to maintain a higher rental income.

Some owners may hear about a two-bedroom unit somewhere renting for $400.00 per month and assume that all two-bedroom units rent for $400.00 per month. There are many variables that determine the maximum rent potential. I have mentioned location and parking, which are important but not necessarily the only value-related amenities. The overall condition of the property is very important. (This needs constant attention.) If you don't plan your investment strategy so that a certain percentage of income is put back into your investment property every year, the property will suffer a loss of appeal that will increase every year it is neglected.

WORKING WITH REAL ESTATE AGENTS

If you have to work with a real estate agent, you need to make sure you are working with an experienced real estate agent who truly understands the market and how to actually negotiate deals, and who can work on your behalf.

We believe in working with agents and believe that the commission that we pay on the properties we purchase is worth their expertise. You will pay the same commission if you work with an experienced agent or an agent who just started working. Our experience, after working with so many different agents, is that you should truly work with the best.

When we call a new area or a real estate office, we've noticed that the calls are answered and passed on round-robin to different agents in the queue. It's rare that the first agent suggested to us is the top agent in the office. We've worked with so many real estate agents that we have started to notice a pattern when we walk into different real estate offices: real estate agents seem to compete in a similar manner as employees at any sales agency. There are top-performing agents and low-performing agents, and offices have pictures or plaques for top agents. In addition, different real estate agents specialize in different markets—something to keep in mind when interviewing different agents.

We have developed a strict policy if we're going to be working with a real estate agent. We only work with one of the top five agents in the office. When we decide to work with a real estate office, we typically make a couple of different calls to that office. In our first call we typically do not discuss why we are calling; we call and ask for the names of the top real estate agents or we walk into the office and ask the same questions. We only want to work with the best in the office. We do not sign any exclusive agreements for any reason until we are convinced that we are working with the right person. In addition, we try to work with real estate agents as buyer's agents only on a non-exclusive basis, and request that the commission be paid from the seller's commission, since the commission is typically split between the agents. We have no problems making this happen.

BAD PROPERTY MANAGERS: WHEN TO REPLACE YOUR PROPERTY MANAGEMENT COMPANY

I have heard a lot of people talk about property managers—some love them and some cannot understand their value. Since we have stated working with property managers, we have replaced a number of management companies and we have chosen not to invest in areas where we could not find a good property management company. For us, the relationship between the property owner and the property manager is a business relationship of mutual respect.

Both parties are benefiting from the business relationship, and from that the personal relationship that can develop.

Some indicators that your property management relationship is not working and you need to consider alternatives include:

- Lack of communication and responsiveness
- Not providing monthly reports and statements
- Lack of understanding of the current market trends, which is connected wit the ability to help you manage and rent your property
- Lack of honesty in communications
- Conflict of interest—for example, if the property manager is managing too many properties owned by the real estate company and your property is not their priority
- The property management company you are working with keeps changing the managers you work with due to turnover
- The property management company cannot find contractors to help you manage your expenses at a reasonable rate
- Lack of understanding of and obedience to local laws
- Lack of responsiveness and hands-on management of tenants—tenant pro lems should not become your problem

Our recommendation to consider replacing your property management company should not be based on only one of the above factors. If you have problems with any one of the above factors, our recommendation is to communicate with your property manager without delay—and, if possible, set up a face-to-face meeting to address issues in a non-confrontational mode.

TYPES OF RELATIONSHIPS THAT WE HAVE BUILT OVER THE YEARS

Over our years of investing, we have built a network of support personnel that we can reach out to when we need to conduct our business. Our philosophy includes trying to use local resources in the area where we've invested and supporting the local economy. At times we have options to go with non-local resources, and we can save a couple of dollars, but in situations like this we have always chosen to support the local economy.

Through our effort to support the local economy, an interesting side effect appeared. By using local resources (contractors, real estate agents, etc.) who understood how things got done in that area and what needed to happen to move things forward, we got things done faster and we got a lot of advice about what we needed to do. It became a win-win situation for us. In addition, we've learned about local events and fun places to visit.

Our current support network includes connections across different geographical regions, such as:

- Real estate agents
- Property managers
- Contractors
- Insurance agents
- Lawyers
- Tax accountants
- Banks
- Law firms
- Title companies
- Shop owners
- Home inspectors

COUPLES' ACTION SUMMARY

Follow your instinct in building relationship with people. They will be helping you manage your properties, so you need to ensure you can trust your support network.

One of the hardest things about building our investment portfolio is working with people and figuring out how to best to deal with the situations that arise. As we have mentioned earlier, one of our most important relationships and one that was key to our success was working with the right property management company. It took us time to find the right relationship. One thing that we strongly recommend is that you do your homework when trying to identify the right management company to help you manage your investments. We recommend that you take the time to interview multiple property management companies prior to finalizing your decision about who to work with. I would recommend that you treat hiring a property manager the same way you would if you were trying to find a good financial advisor or a good tax accountant. We could say that you should do your due diligence as if you were hiring an employee, but we believe that a property manager is more like a business partner—but a very important one.

When choosing a property management company, we have been most successful working with small businesses and locally owned real estate and property management companies. We have found that working with a smaller realty company, you typically get more dedicated service, and employees work harder to earn your business. Some of them are very particular about who they work with, and we welcome this since it means that if we pass muster our business will be getting a lot of individual attention.

We recommend that, as a couple, both of you need to interview the property management companies, and the decision about whom to work with needs to be mutual, since you will both need to work with the property management company from time to time.

NOTES

TASKS

☐

☐

☐

☐

☐

☐

☐

☐

☐

CHAPTER EIGHT

PLANNING AND IMPLEMENTING A GROWTH STRATEGY: LET'S GO

Have a target and put a short-term and long-term strategy into effect as you work toward achieving your goals

- As a couple, what are your future expectations?
- Do you know what monthly income you will need in the future?
- What is the necessary growth strategy in order to achieve your goals?
- What are your five-year, ten-year, and fifteen-year objectives?
- What is your pie in the sky? Ours is owning fifty properties in fifteen years, generating at least $30K of passive income per month. The question: is that achievable? And what planning do we need to do in order to achieve it?
- If done right, our investment can be passed from generation to generation, helping our children and their children achieve their goals through our hard work.

THE EIGHT-STEP APPROACH TO GETTING STARTED WITH YOUR FIRST PROPERTY

GETTING STARTED

You have made it this far in reading this book. Now let's look at putting everything together and get ready to make it fun. As a family, we have had a lot of fun and many adventures making this happen. We hope you can do the same.

So far in this book, we have covered a lot of different topics to provide you with some background information about our approach and strategy.

Once you have an understanding of your spending habits and have implemented ways to manage your spending, you are on your way to getting started. The rest of this book contains information about the details of some of the steps that you will need to take. Our recommendation is that you read through the rest of the book prior to executing the steps in this chapter.

The eight steps to getting started are:

- Step 1 – Understand your long-term objectives—the endgame
- Step 2 – Develop your growth strategy and an initial investment budget
- Step 3 – Research the areas where you're interested in investing
- Step 4 – Reach out to property managers/real estate agents in these areas
- Step 5 – Tour the areas
- Step 6 – Create a Limited Liability Company (LLC)
- Step 7 – Select a number of properties for analysis
- Step 8 – Place an offer, close the deal, and get ready to make passive income

STEP 1 – UNDERSTAND YOUR LONG-TERM OBJECTIVES: THE ENDGAME

Both of us work very hard in our day-to-day lives. We often talk about the uncertainties in our future and what needs to be done to ensure that we have what we need for the long term. We all work and save so that, when we retire, we will have enough to live on. We are so thankful that we have jobs now and we can save some money, but we keep looking forward into the future to try to predict uncertainties and what kind of financial security we'll need to meet them. We have read a lot of books and articles, as well as used many of the formulas utilized by financial advisors, to get an idea of how much money we need to have in the bank when we retire or what type of returns we need to have in place.

If you look at social security, pension funds, and 401(k), as well as the stock markets and pure saving accounts, none of these options provide you with a monthly cash flow that would be enough to sustain you for the long haul. Traditional philosophies focus on a person retiring at the age of sixty-five with a nest egg, and utilizing that nest egg to live the rest of their life. Both of our parents are in that situation. Their only source of income is their savings, and they have had to dramatically change their lifestyles and manage budgets and monthly spending since they have no way to replenish what they spend. Oftentimes, we push them to take an extra vacation or travel, but now that they are retired, they are very budget-conscious and concerned about spending. When CJ pushes his dad, his dad always says, "At least you are working—if you spend it, you have time to rebuild your savings. All we have is our savings." As we grow older, traditional saving approaches make us feel like we are running out of time.

We hear it time after time from our older friends: they can't afford to retire and they have to continue working to ensure that when they do retire they can maintain the same lifestyle that they have today. The sad part is that today, most people feel that they need to work until they are sixty-eight or seventy years old. There's nothing wrong with working as you grow older, but in our opinion it should be an option and at that age working should be pursued for fun, not out of necessity.

If you want to see the reality of this for yourself, try searching the Internet for retirement calculators. Every calculator will collect some information from you at the start—typical questions include your current age, current annual income, desired retirement age, desired retirement income, life expectancy, expected annual pension, and expected Social Security income. You will be amazed and shocked how much money you need to have saved in the bank when you retire if you have no additional income supplementing your current income. In addition, you will be amazed at the cost of insurance per month once you do not have coverage through your employer. As an example, if you are forty-one years old and plan to retire at sixty-five, and you make around $120K per year, with a life expectancy of eighty-five, most calculators will tell you that you need $3.1-3.6 million (taking inflation into account—that's about $1.7 million in today's money) in savings in order to maintain your lifestyle. In looking at both of our parents and most of the people we know who are at retirement age, they haven't saved anywhere near that much money—life has thrown them curveballs along the way and they've had to make tough decisions that did not allow them to build up that kind of savings.

In our opinion, relying only on savings accounts, Social Security, and pensions is not the way you should plan for the future. You need to consider having a continuous source of income that will replace your current income and provide you the freedom you need. We believe investing in real estate should be a major component of your investment portfolio, in part because the income it generates can help supplement other retirement income.

We can approach this from another angle and look at how much annual income you will need when you retire, using a conservative estimate and assuming you will need 80% of your current income per year. If you currently make $100K combined income, this means you will need $80K per year or $6.6K per month. If you have rental units that provide you on average $650 per month each after expenses, then you would need seven to twelve units fully paid off by the time you retire. You can always sell one of the units in the future if you need more cash. After 12 years of investing and working hard, we have achieved our goals. At this stage, we have time to look back and fix what is needed while we continue our investment strategies to reach our target of 50 units before we reach our retirement age.

STEP 2 – DEVELOP YOUR GROWTH STRATEGY AND AN INITIAL INVESTMENT BUDGET

One of the first steps toward determining your growth strategy is developing an understanding of what the strategy needs to be. For the sake of simplicity and in order to establish a baseline, let's look at the steps that we took when we were trying to understand what we needed:

- Look at your current monthly income to determine your future needs
- Look at the number of properties that will be needed to achieve that goal
- Look at your goals to achieve stability—five-year, ten-year, and fifteen-year goals.
- Look into estimated property purchase price as well as potential property income. Base the price on your research within a 2-4 hour drive of the area that you want to invest in or retire in.
- ? Estimate the number of properties that will be needed to provide you that income, as well as some of the budgets that will be needed.
- ★ Based on what you can save per year, and available funds, determine what type of strategy is needed

- You do not need to worry about future inflation costs; the assumption is that the rental income will rise with inflation

To further expand on the above, we will make the following assumptions:

- ★ A working couple, where each person makes a minimum of $80K per year, or a combined income of $160K per year
- ★ An income of $160K per year implies that household monthly income is $13K per month before taxes
- ★ You have developed an understanding of what percent of your combined income you would like to have at retirement. Look at your portfolio and then determine what is the rental return per property.
- ★ With a ten-year plan to achieve your goals, you will then have an understanding of the target number of properties needed to achieve the goal ove time. For example, if each unit had an average return of $800 per month, then you would need to own about sixteen units (the return being considered is after expenses)

Now that you have an idea of how many properties you may need, you can look at your combined income in order to determine how much to save and how much you need to allocate each month in order to get started. We started slow, one property per year, and then we increased the number.

- ★ An income of $160K per year implies monthly income of around $9.5K after taxes.
- ★ Assume house expenses and the cost of living can be managed with around $5.5K per month. You can potentially have around $4K to save for investing. That is, you can save $48K per year and put it toward investments. If you have extra income, you can apply more

of that income to your savings; any extra money, such as bonuses, gifts, and what we call "found money" goes into that account.

- ★ You really need to be aggressive in your savings. At times we limit and manage our expenses very tightly for three to four months in order to achieve or exceed our savings goal for that period.
- ★ Given the ability to save $48K per year for investment, you can start by getting mortgages on the first couple of properties and have an aggressive schedule to pay them off by using the monthly income generated, as well as your monthly savings.

Once the first properties are paid off, the monthly income is added to the savings account for investment, and the cycle continues. Your ability to pay off the properties wil depend on the cost of the properties that are within your target investment area. In addition to income, you can take into account other ways to generate the initial or baseline equity to allow you to kick-start your investment strategies. For us, it was the sale of our first house. Taking the profits as the baseline of our investment funding, coupled with our saving strategies and target investment areas, has allowed us to adjust our strategy on a yearly basis as we continue to invest and grow our portfolio. Once you have an understanding of your approach to funding your investments, then you can use that as a baseline as part of the next step (Step 3) for your research.

STEP 3 – RESEARCH THE AREAS WHERE YOU'RE INTERESTED IN INVESTING: THE POWER OF THE INTERNET

In previous chapters we have talked about road trips and exploring different places while you're touring the areas you might invest in. We recommend that you start looking in a two to three-hour driving radius from where you currently live. The first area that we invested in—Cumberland, Maryland—we happened to find by mistake. During one of our mini-trips to an area called Deep Creek Lake, we drove by a town that appeared to be filled with historic buildings. On our way back, we decided to stop by the town and were impressed by the people and the architecture.

Later, when we decided to start looking at different areas where we might begin our real estate investment, Cumberland was one of two areas (Williamsport, Pennsylvania, being the other) that we decided to invest in, following a lot of research on our part.

There are many ways you can start your search for properties. Today, with the Internet, particularly sites like Zillow.com and Redfin.com, you have a lot of power to understand real estate markets without driving anywhere. Zillow.com offers tools that allow you to start from your address and zoom to the different areas so you can understand the prices in different neighborhoods around you. As an example, with Zillow, you can look at a map for a given area with all the houses for sale, as well as estimated values for properties and the estimated rent for given properties in the area.

Our recommendation is that you examine areas within driving distance from your home or ask family and friends about their favorite areas within driving distance. Start your market search there.

STEP 4 – REACH OUT TO PROPERTY MANAGERS / REAL ESTATE AGENTS IN THESE AREAS

Once you have decided which areas/locations you want to research because it may make sense to invest there, we recommend making a property manager or real estate agent your tour guide.

We've found it's very helpful, when exploring a new area, to contact a real estate agent ahead of our visit and scheduling time to look at different properties. It's also great if you can search online for local property management companies and schedule some time to meet with them while you're visiting.

When we first visited Williamsport, Pennsylvania, we really didn't know much at all about the area other than what we'd found online. When we met with Tom, our real estate agent, who had always lived in Williamsport, we really got a different feel and appreciation for the area. For one thing, Tom was able to tell us about all the different attractions in the area, including the Little League baseball event that Williamsport hosts every season, the nearby universities and colleges, the parks and tourist attractions, and the wineries within driving distance. He also gave us an up-close look by touring the different areas of the city with us and telling us which neighborhoods we might want to stay away from because of high crime rates. This was really helpful for us as we looked at different properties for potential investment. Tom was also helpful in giving us an idea about the price fluctuation in the area and the overall trends in home prices. As a real estate agent, he had access to a lot of different properties that we didn't find online, and he helped us find the property that worked for us based on our ROI formula.

There are several reasons why you'd want to reach out to a property management company even before you purchase a property in the area. First of all, you want to make sure that there is a reliable property management company that can take care of the daily operations and get your property rented. Secondly, it's important to know what you can expect in rental income from the property you're considering buying. The real estate agent can give you a high-level idea of the potential rent, and you can get a general idea of the rental market in the area by looking at online resources such as City-Data.com—but the best way to gauge your potential rental income is to have the company that will be managing your rental property walk through it and provide you with a more accurate number based on the property's condition, location, and current demand for rentals in the area. In addition, the property management company can provide you with a detailed list of the items that you'd need to address in order to rent the property, giving you a good cost estimate of maintenance costs and other out-of-pocket expenses to get the property rented. This will help you in negotiating down the price if you decide to make an offer on a property.

STEP 5 – TOUR THE AREAS

When we're considering investing in a new area, we always make it a point to visit and stay in the area at least a couple of times before we put an offer down on a property. This step is very important for us because we only like to invest in areas where we would consider staying and living. In other words, if we don't fall in love with the area after staying there, chances are we won't be investing in it. Since we're investing our hard-earned money and betting our future on this investment, it's important for us to feel comfortable in the area where we buy our rental properties.

Even though you can get a lot of information about the area online by checking different web sites and visiting city and tourism sites about the area, it's never quite the same as actually staying there. Because most of our investment areas are within a three-hour driving distance, we usually plan a long weekend trip to go and explore the area. We rely on our real estate agent or property manager to recommend things we should do and places we should visit while there, but we also follow our sense of adventure.

One of the things we always do is pick up the local magazines and real estate sales booklets from the hotel lobby. We go through them thoroughly to understand the major point of interests in the area and also to get a better look at the real estate market. This helps us be better prepared when we talk to a real estate agent. In addition, we often find things we want to do while in the area by reading these magazines. For example, there may be local farmer's markets, flea markets, festivals, or antique shows that we want to check out during our stay.

Another way we explore the town is by talking to local residents. We typically go to local shops and talk to the owners to get their thoughts about the area. We go to grocery stores to understand where the major shopping outlets are. We try to locate major points of interest that could affect the rental potential of our property: proximity to shopping, restaurants, hospitals, schools, universities, public transportation, and businesses. We also try to understand what drives the local economy to develop a better understanding of the future economic viability of the area we are considering investing in.

STEP 6 – CREATE A LIMITED LIABILITY COMPANY (LLC)

You should consider creating an LLC if you're able to buy a property without having a mortgage. A bank will not finance or provide a traditional mortgage on a property in the name of the LLC. If you plan to get a mortgage on your first properties, you can skip Step 6 and continue on to Step 7.

Creating an LLC in an important step to ensure you are protecting your current assets from any liabilities that may arise due to renting a property. The LLC will help protect your other financial investments outside real estate investments. If a property is in the name of the LLC and you are sued for any reason, the extent of your liability will be the financials that are owned and managed by the LLC. If you decide to create an LLC, you have a wide range of online resources that can help in creating one.

We did not set up an LLC when we started our investments, since we did not know about it nor understand the value of protecting ourselves in this way. What triggered us looking at liability and our various options is that we had one of our tenants put an above-ground swimming pool on our property without our knowledge. During one of the backyard parties at the property, the cops and our property manager were called to deal with loud noice. Even though we did not have an incident, and the tenant did not ask for permission, we wanted to look at the options available to help protect our investment.

Many people have advised us that we should have multiple LLCs and combine our properties under multiple LLCs to limit our liability. The recommendation is that each rental property should be in its own LLC. Today we have established a number of LLCs to help protect the different investments that we have.

In terms of LLC accounting affecting your taxes, your tax accountant can explain your options to you. If you plan to take a mortgage on your properties, you should talk to your lender about the best approach to financing the properties through the LLC. Working with an LLC will require more lead time and may require different documentation, depending on the transaction, so it is important to consider this early on when planning your investments.

STEP 7 – SELECT A NUMBER OF PROPERTIES FOR ANALYSIS

Once you have chosen the area where you want to invest, it's important to look at the available real estate inventory and select a number of properties that you may want to consider for further evaluation. Once you have narrowed down the list of potential properties, you need to schedule a walk-through for each property.

The way we approach this step is by looking at the following factors:

PRICE

Cash-flow management is an important factor for supporting your strategy of growing your investments. Price is very important if you're planning to buy with cash, since the less cash you spend the more cash you will have for repairs and future investments. When we're considering different properties we always stick to a price range that we're comfortable with. This quickly narrows down your options and allows you to focus your research on affordable properties where the numbers make sense for you. When you're considering price, it's also important to understand the reason why the property is listed for sale and your ability to negotiate the price down accordingly. For example, is this an estate sale, a divorce sale, a short sale or bank-owned property?

TYPE OF PROPERTY

Ever since we started investing, we have only purchased duplexes or single-family homes for our investment properties. By sticking to this model, we've been able to manage our risk and vacancy. It's important to determine the type of property you wish to invest in, because this will help narrow down your investment options.

LOCATION

This is a very important factor to consider, as location can determine whether you can get the property rented, and the income it may generate. Wherever you choose to invest, there will be good and bad neighborhoods, and you'll want to stay away from some streets because of high crime rates. It's important to talk to a property management company that really knows the area you're investing in and assess the neighborhood before you make an offer on any property.

RENTAL POTENTIAL

Since your main goal is to generate passive income from your investment and to recover your initial cost in six or seven years, it's very important to understand the expected monthly rent that a property can generate before you make an offer. The best way to get a real estimate of the rental potential is to ask the property management company that would be taking care of the investment for you to provide an assessment based on the property's condition, location, and rental demand in the area. This allows you to understand if the numbers truly make sense and if the property meets your ROI formula.

TAXES

It's important to look at the taxes on a property before you make a decision to invest in it. For example, some areas will have historic taxes, city taxes, and school taxes in addition to state taxes. These taxes can easily add up and negatively impact your bottom line. To ensure profitability on your investment, you need to take this factor into consideration before you make an offer on any property.

UTILITIES

Utilities are another important factor to consider, since they will affect your bottom line. If the property is a single-family home, it's easy to assume that the tenant will pay for all utilities. However, the situation can get more complicated if you are investing in a duplex, for example, and there's no separate water heater for each unit. In those cases, it's typically the landlord who pays these utilities and then charges rent accordingly to cover the related expenses. The other point to consider is the type of utility used for heat. In some areas, oil heat can get really expensive during the winter months. You may want to consider staying away from investing in a property that relies on oil heat, especially if you believe that potential tenants may default on paying their heating bills during the winter months. Remember that as a landlord, you'll always be responsible for paying the bill—this holds true when a tenant defaults and when the property is vacant.

PROXIMITY TO MAJOR POINTS OF INTEREST

Before you make the decision to invest in a property, you need to consider what could make a potential tenant decide to rent your unit rather than another one on the market. Proximity to schools, universities, hospitals, businesses, public transportation, play areas, shopping centers, or restaurants can all play a major role in making your property more attractive and can get you better rent, especially in a competitive rental market.

PROPERTY CONDITION

When considering a property, we always try to assess the cost of getting it ready for rental. In most cases, we try to avoid any properties that require major renovation work to get them rented. If the work is mostly cosmetic (such as painting, putting in new carpets, etc.), then it's typically a good investment for us. By having a property management company walk through the property, you can get a detailed list of what needs to be fixed before the property can take new tenants. This will help you estimate your cost of renovation and maintenance in the future. In addition, you need to consider the general layout of the property, including:

- Does the flow from one room to another make ense?
- How many bedrooms and bathrooms does it have?
- If it has a basement, do you want to make it accessible to tenants?
- Does it have a backyard or safe play area for kids?
- Does it have a porch or deck?
- Most importantly, would you live in the house?
- What would you change if you were going to live there?

PARKING AVAILABILITY

This is very important, especially if your property is not close to public transportation and you believe that your tenants will have one or more cars. We have several properties that don't have driveways or garages, but before we make a decision on a property we always check the availability of on-street parking. If it's not a busy street, it's usually acceptable and safe for most tenants, even those with kids and large families. However, if the property is on a busy street where it's often hard to find an on-street parking spot close to the house, it becomes a potential problem, especially if your tenants have children.

STEP 8 – PLACE AN OFFER, CLOSE THE DEAL, AND GET READY TO MAKE PASSIVE INCOME

Once you have looked at the different factors mentioned in the previous step and researched in detail the list of potential investment properties, it's easy to make a decision on which one is the best option for you.

The next step is to make an offer on that property and start the negotiation process. One of the things we always ask our agent is why the property is listed for sale. If it's an estate sale, a divorce sale, a short sale, or a bank-owned property, you can typically negotiate the price down significantly and bring down your initial investment.

It's also important to understand the market. In a buyer's market, your negotiation power is much higher than in a seller's market. In general, when we make an offer on a property, we never start with more than 75% of its listing price, regardless of the market.

Another point to keep in mind is that if you're paying cash, you can usually negotiate more. Once you have made an offer, the seller will either accept it or come back with a counteroffer. If they do, be willing to respond with a counteroffer, but know beforehand the most you're willing to pay for the property, and don't go beyond that number, because it will affect your profitability and mess with your ROI formula.

Once you have agreed on the price and terms with the seller, get ready to close the deal and start working on your property with the management company to prepare it for rental.

COUPLES' ACTION SUMMARY

Our aggressive dual income strategy: one partner's income is for us to live on, while the other partner's income is used only for investment.

A lot of folks that advise you to invest say you should use "other peoples' money" to invest. Our philosophy is a bit different: "Use your employers' money to invest." In other words, we work today to secure our future. We have to work long enough to save enough to secure our future based on our plan; afterward, our goal is to work because we want to work. If both spouses are working, which is the case with most people we know, we strongly recommend you look at whose income can be used as the investment vehicle and what you can do to modify your lifestyle so you can support yourselves on one person's income while the other's is used for investments.

continued

COUPLES' ACTION SUMMARY

- Finding the right property requires that you take a look at a large number of properties and narrow them down based on your criteria; establish your criteria list and know what type property you want to look for
- Research, research, research—you need to research your target market and the property manager that will help you through this process
- Every week we spend two to four hours looking at properties ourselves—we do not depend on others to find properties for us

If we find a property where the numbers work for us, we reach out to the different property managers we are working with and ask them to research further for us. A lot of the properties we've purchased are ones we found by ourselves first.

This chapter is an important chapter because it helps you define your strategy and approach to investment. We recommend that after you finish reading this book, you come back as a couple and review the different steps mentioned in this chapter over a cup of coffee or your favorite drinks—review it in a relaxing environment and talk as a couple about how best to put a plan of action in place and move it forward.

NOTES

NOTES

TASKS

- [ ]
- [ ]
- [ ]
- [ ]
- [ ]
- [ ]
- [ ]
- [ ]
- [ ]

CHAPTER NINE

TO BUY OR NOT TO BUY: MAKING A GO/NO-GO DECISION

One of the most important things for succeeding in real estate investment is putting your money in the right property. Once you have determined the area you want to invest in, you need to ensure you find the right property management company to help you with your efforts.

- Understanding what type of property works best in terms of return on investment
- Considering flips: Not for a long-term investment plan
- Understanding the importance of location, price, cost, and "rentability"
- Searching for curb appeal: The property needs to pass the "Yucky" test

CHOOSING THE RIGHT PROPERTY: WHAT TYPE OF PROPERTY SHOULD YOU INVEST IN?

DUE DILIGENCE

Attention to detail and investing the time to research a property is critical. Taking shortcuts or rushing through the decision-making process can be costly. You need to establish a system that will help you assess your budget and ROI for a given property prior to making the go decision. Not understanding your budget prior to investment can result in many challenges.

We would like to start by saying we currently invest only in single or double-family homes. This is not necessarily the right option for everyone, but we have found this works best for us. Some of our doubles are deeded separately and we have the option of selling them individually in the future, but as a principle we only invest in single/double units and we invest for the long term. We do not go in for flips or any other form of investments.

Why do we only invest in single or double units?

- With these properties, you can have the tenant pay for full utilities. Most multiple units we have looked at required the investor to pay for the utilities and then include them as part of the monthly rent. We have found it more difficult to rent a place in which you include utilities in the price, both from the investor perspective and the tenant perspective. The tenant, by managing the cost of electricity, heat, and gas can reduce their own cost. For the investor, if utilities are all part of the monthly cost, tenants can abuse the utilities and managing the monthly cash flow from the property can become difficult. In addition, you do not have to worry about fluctuations in the utilities prices or having to factor that into your ROI estimation.
- Investing in singles and doubles is a form of investment diversification. If we make a mistake on a property and it is a single or a double, it is easier to sell than if you have an apartment building.
- With a double, you only need to worry about two tenants getting along. We have heard about many difficulties managing tenants from people who own multi-unit apartments.
- With single and double units, you can get a larger living space for families, and in most of our properties we can offer a backyard for kids and pets.
- Single and double units seem to appreciate more in terms of value over the long term. Double units are attractive for a lot of first-time investors who are looking to live in one unit and rent the other.

- The property managers we've worked with tend to prefer managing one or two-unit properties for ease of management.

Other types of real estate investment, such as condos, townhomes, seasonal units, three and four-unit buildings, apartment complexes, and commercial investments are options people can pursue. When we first started investing we were not sure exactly what to invest in. We had options on where to start investing; we were qualified to borrow a good amount of money, up to $800K. One thing was sure, though: we wanted to be conservative about how much debt we took on, since we were not 100% sure about how it would all work out. After investing in single units, duplexes, and multi-unit/commercial properties, we have adjusted our portfolio to just have single and double units. We found other types of properties hard to manage even when working with a property management company. Over the past twelve years, we have stuck to what we know best, single units and duplexes, and so far that has worked well for us.

AVOIDING THE FLIP

Though we have been investing in real estate for several years now, we have avoided working on properties just to flip them. That was never part of our investment strategy for a number of reasons. One of the most important ones is that CJ is fascinated with reality shows in which people flip properties. We loved watching people on TV go through houses, rip them apart and deal with all the challenges that come with the flip. Once the house is ready and the renovations are done, you have to worry about how to market, stage, and sell the house for a profit. One of the simplest observations we've made from watching these shows and reading a couple of books about flips is that you need time, attention, and full dedication to the project to be successful. With all the experience we have now taking on properties, I am sure we could easily buy a property and flip it, but we don't do it because we have day jobs and we do not have the support of a property management company. In addition, in the markets where we invest, you can make maybe $10-30K per flip, if you do it right. But you have to take a lot of things into account; many people don't understand the true challenge of working on a property and managing renovations yourself until they have gone through it. You also have to deal with the tax implications of a flip. We have bought a number of properties from owners who intended to flip them but went way over budget. Not all flips are successful, whatever you may see on TV.

Most of us who own houses have remodeled a bathroom, upgraded a kitchen, or just added carpets or hardwood floors. If you have tried any one of these simple remodels and you think coordinating with contractors, suppliers, and others is a challenge, imagine how much harder a true flip would be. This is not to say that we have not renovated any of our properties ourselves—we have done our share of the work and realized that we are not experts on the fixer-upper side. We now rely on our property management companies to bring in the right people and get the job done. If you have the right relationship with the right contractor, you might be able to make flips work, but we don't recommend flips because they do not fit into our long-term investment strategy for passive income generation, and we do not want to invest our precious free time in projects that will derail our investment strategies.

THE STREET OR NEIGHBORHOOD DRIVE

It still amazes us how neighborhoods in the same area can differ so much in price and in how many people want to live there. In certain areas, the differences can be by section of a given street. That is, if you drive down one street, you can see a whole series of houses that are very nicely maintained, and then you reach part of the street where lawns are not maintained, houses are boarded up or need painting, junky cars are parked on the lawns, etc. The difference can be night and day. Sometimes when we are researching an area, someone will tell us to make sure the property we're looking at on a certain street has a street number above 500, if we want any tenants.

Real estate agents and property managers have strict laws about what they can say about a given neighborhood. The information about a given area is always given to us from a high level, and we have to make our own decision based on whether the property falls within our investment criteria. We are only looking at the property from a business and marketability point of view.

When we are looking at a property we might invest in, we look at the houses at least four to six houses to the right and the left of the property, as well as properties on the other side of the street. These are some of the things we look for:

- Are the homes well maintained, in terms of paint, etc.? Do we see signs that owners/tenants take pride in the homes?
- Are any of the homes boarded up/abandoned?
- Are the lawns well maintained?
- How clean are the streets? Can we see garbage in the streets?
- How clean and well maintained are the houses on the drive-by to the property?
- Generally, would we feel safe driving kids through the neighborhoods to get to the property?
- Is there any graffiti on the walls or the street?
- Are there kids playing in the streets or on the lawns? Does it seem like a happy neighborhood?

From the drive-by in a given neighborhood, you can tell a lot about the area. This drive-by gives you an understanding beyond just looking at a listing on the Web or on paper. Most of our properties were forgotten properties in great neighborhoods. In fact, when we are done working on our properties, the neighbors are very happy that we own the properties. We pay a lot of attention to making ours one of the better properties on the street. We invest in our properties to ensure that they remain that way.

LOCATION, CURB APPEAL, AND THE NATALIE "YUCKY" TEST

Beyond the neighborhood appeal, the next important factor in our property evaluation is the curb appeal of the property. We devote a substantial part of our renovation budget to ensuring we make a good first impression on a potential tenant. We invest in planting flowers, adding a little character to the front porch, painting the front doors, and so on. We've learned that the little touches that show a tenant you care about how your property looks make them strive to maintain your property better. If your tenant believes that you do not care about the property, they will not care about it either.

Today, as we continue to move forward with our investment strategy, we travel as a family and we look at investment properties with our kids. We started this tradition early on; when we traveled to look at properties it was a family event for us. When Natalie was three years old, we had noticed that she was listening to us discuss the different properties. During one of our property tours with Natalie, out of the blue she started sharing her opinions about the property, telling us if the house was "yucky" or if she liked it. We have come to take her opinion on a property's curb appeal into consideration. Today we take both Natalie and Danny on our trips and we ask them for their opinion.

It may seem silly that we are listening to our young children on investment decisions, but for us it has made the decision-making process more fun and helped us stay closer as a family.

When we look at properties, we do not expect a property to have full curb appeal from day one, but we have to see the potential of the property.

THE PROPERTY WALK-THROUGH: ESTIMATING THE TRUE COST

Making a decision about purchasing a property is always hard, especially since you are investing your money, time, and effort and banking that you can turn the investment around for a profit. If you work hard for your money, this is not an easy decision. Over the years, we have become much better at understanding what to look for in a property and how to assess what it would take to get it ready for the rental market. One day during a road trip to Cumberland, we were discussing some of the challenges of our properties and the amount of time it took to get some properties rented. Out of the blue, Jinan said, "Knock a wall down and you add three to five months to your renovation project." CJ's answer, after thinking about it, was, "So true," and we started laughing about it.

Today, we use that wisdom when making decisions about the purchase or renovation of a property. If, in looking at a given property, we decide that after purchase we would like to knock a wall down to make it more rentable, then we will need to factor the time into our estimate of when the property will be ready for market. Over the years, we have done some renovations ourselves, hired skilled contractors, hired unskilled contractors, worked with construction companies, managed a full renovation project, and subcontracted some renovation projects. The major lesson we learned is to have a strong property manager who is experienced with managing renovation efforts and let him or her run with it. Property managers typically work with their own crew to manage and maintain properties or they have a list of trusted and reliable subcontractors that they use on a regular basis. Our experience has taught us that, due to the volume of work property managers provide to the group of contractors they work with, we typically get competitive bids and good service without having to be very involved in the daily renovation process.

It is important to note that you need to have a renovation budget prior to purchasing a property. If not managed properly, renovations can become very costly very fast. Over the years, we have developed a basic system that helps us understand the cost of renovation. The cost estimate of the renovations starts with the initial walk-through of the house, either by us or the property manager. The walk-through involves walking through every room in the property and taking pictures and making notes about the minimum amount of work necessary to get the property rented. We always keep in mind another one of our core principles: "Any property that we rent, we have to be willing to live in it after we finish the renovation." Given that, the minimum amount of work has to meet a pretty high standard.

Looking at what shape a property's in is a big step for us in deciding to move forward with the possibility of investing or just walk away.

There are a number of things that would make us walk away from a given property:

- Illegal additions to the property
- A property that is currently rented illegally
- The property floor plan does not make sense and major remodeling is needed
- Floors or walls do not appear to be straight, suggesting that the property might have foundation problems
- Heating/furnace units are oil based, or it appears the unit needs a brand-new heater/furnace

- The foundation of the house seems to be unstable
- The house's electric wiring needs to be replaced
- The property needs total renovation—that means you need to replace plumbing, wiring, walls, etc. This can be very expensive, with a lot of unknowns and hidden issues. The risk of taking on a project like this is too high for us.

If the property doesn't have any of the above issues, we start by looking at different factors to determine if the property is a good investment for us. The property walk-through is a major component of our purchase analysis. As part of our walk-through we pay close attention to the following:

Windows: How old are the windows? Do they need replacement? Older windows or out-of-shape windows, such as windows that are broken or damaged, will cause a lot of issues for your tenants and bring the heating/cooling bills up. This can cause a high turnover rate and increase your vacancy cost in the long run.

Water leaks: As you walk through the house, look closely for water leaks. If you don't address the root cause of leaks, they can cause mold and can be very expensive to fix later on.

Termites: We always have the property inspected for termites before or after the purchase, even if we buy a property as is. We strongly recommend a termite inspection.

Mold: If you notice a lot of water damage in the property, you may need to consider inspecting for mold. If the property has mold, this can be very costly to fix.

Asbestos: A lot of older homes have asbestos in them. This may be an issue with properties, especially in the basements if the piping is covered with asbestos and they are not fully covered or sealed. This can create additional costs you hadn't planned for.

Lead paint: Older homes tend to have lead paint, and most areas have regulations for lead paint management in order to protect tenants. We typically budget $300-500 per property to ensure lead paint inspection is being addressed.

Radon gas: We have noticed that some areas are known for radon gas issues. We walked away from one of our first properties because a radon gas inspection revealed that the property was unsafe due to the radon levels. We could have worked to fix the issue, but we decided not to move forward.

Electricity and wiring: Look at the house's wiring—does it need updating? We decided not to buy one house out of fear of the electric rewiring cost. The house looked very nice from the outside; we remember the property vividly since this was part of our search for our third investment property. The tenant that was renting one of the units had three ferrets running around the house as we were doing the walk-through. There were extension cords running from room to room in order to get electricity to different parts of the house. The tenant indicated that most outlets did not work and that she had informed the landlord about it. We decided that the cost of rewiring was going to be too high and that the house was a big risk for us, so we walked away.

Heating type: We tend to shy away from any home that has electric or oil heat. We have realized that in both cases heating becomes very expensive for our tenants and prices fluctuate significantly from month to month depending on the weather. These heating systems also tend to generate more issues than gas heat.

Roof conditions: When buying a house, we always try to figure out when and if the roof was changed, and we always have the roof inspected either before or after the sale even if we buy a property as is. A leaky roof can be very expensive, especially if your tenant does not inform you of the leak.

Bathrooms: Bathrooms are major components of any rental. We pay very close attention to the location and condition of each. Most of the earlier properties that we purchased had only one bathroom, typically on the second floor of the units. Today, when we look at a property like this, we factor into our renovation budget the cost of adding a second half or full bathroom. This can be expensive.

Kitchens: Kitchens are another major component of a rental unit. The kitchen's openness and ease of access, as well as its modern look and feel, can be very important factors in getting the unit rented.

Washer/dryer hookups: It is important that you examine whether the property has hookups for a washer or dryer.

Heating system condition: If the heating system needs replacement, this is a big expense.

We also look at how we can make our properties more attractive by putting ourselves in the tenant's shoes and taking into consideration the following design and layout options:

- Number of bathrooms and locations of bathrooms
- Washer/dryer hookups
- Kitchen layout
- Room-to-room flow
- Air conditioning

Another very important factor that we look at is the overall neighborhood appeal of the property.

What is the view of the other properties from our property? Does everything look good? For example, one property we purchased looked great from the front and the layout was good, but the main problem was the backyard. Across the street, we were facing the back of a building where the owner stored a lot of junk. We had no control over that, but it made the property unattractive and we knew this could deter potential tenants from using the backyard. That would be a problem if we rented the property to a family with kids or pets. Our solution was to invest in adding a fence to the backyard that was high enough to hide the back of the building, and to plant some trees that would eventually hide the view.

All the above items factor into what you want to tackle as part of the property renovations after purchase. Some renovations can be budgeted for in the long term while others must be addressed immediately in order to rent the unit. Some long-term items include roof replacement, boiler replacement, or window replacements.

Once you understand your renovation costs prior to purchase, you can use that cost as part of the reasoning for price negotiations with the bank or current owner, your property manager, and/or the seller's real estate agent. We have used this technique successfully on a regular basis as part of our price negotiation process.

CJ and I truly use a team approach to assess what each property needs. We enjoy going through a property together and talking through what we'd like to do to take the property to the next level. We can spend a couple of hours walking through a property that we are interested in purchasing. We discuss and document as a team the different things that we would like changed.

Once we have our list, there are two components to consider when putting together a high-level estimate for the project. These two components are materials and labor. We have read some books and talked to property management companies that recommend replacing everything upfront so that you have reduced maintenance costs in the long term. However, we have been able to manage with regular inspections and keeping a maintenance schedule for each property.

CREATING THE HIGH-LEVEL RENOVATION BUDGET

When making a budget, there are some things you should take into account:

Priority tasks and would-be-nice tasks: Try to assign priority to what needs to be done and allocate a budget to cover everything. If you run into issues or unexpected costs, the lower priority or would-be-nice tasks can be removed from the final list.

Material costs: If you do not plan ahead for your materials, they can be costly—not only due to the material purchase prices, but also because of time lost and delays to the delivery date because of lead time on material orders.

Labor costs: Estimating how long a task is going to take in order to determine labor costs can be challenging. You will need to get a labor estimate or a fixed-cost estimate, or else you may run into budget challenges.

Inspections: Depending on the quality of the rental property you're considering, you may want to budget for a boiler inspection, roof inspection, termite inspection, radon inspection, full home inspection, and other inspections you think may be needed.

Time to market: Each month a property is not rented, you are not generating income. You may need to up your budget or hire multiple contractors to work at the same time in order to deliver the property on your intended date.

COUPLES' ACTION SUMMARY

The Importance of Due Diligence:

Once you have chosen an area that you like and would like to invest in, due diligence and attention to detail become very important. You need to stay on top of things, or else you will probably end up losing money.

It is important to work as a team when deciding whether to buy. You should rely on each other's expertise or decide to divide and conquer if needed. For us, the decision to move forward has to be a mutual decision, since in the end both of us will have to deal with the property, and we will both be affected by the success or failure of the property.

You need to work as a team to ensure that the purchase of the property is not an emotional buy, but rather based on your approach, your ROI formula, and your mutual agreement.

Making the decision to move forward requires coordination and agreement by both of you. It requires looking at schedules, as well as discussing how best to move forward. Once our daughter was born, we had to manage our schedules and exercise better time management in order to ensure we had the time necessary to continue investing. This meant working even harder as a team and reassessing who was responsible for what, then moving forward as a team that could respond flexibly to different events in our lives.

NOTES

NOTES

TASKS

CHAPTER TEN

CLOSING THE DEAL

One of the most important things we've learned is that a deal is not closed until the contract is signed

- Understand your power to negotiate the terms of the contract
- Understand how you can leverage the contract to your advantage
- Understand the steps you need to take to get the deal you want while overcoming potential obstacles
- Use a local attorney who understands the local zoning laws and has local connections

THE OFFER: UNDERSTANDING THE CONTRACT OF SALE

> **YOUR GOALS**
>
> Closing the deals one property at a time helps you as a couple reach your ultimate goal. As we look at each property, we do not forget our objectives, why we started investing, and our ultimate goal of financial independence.

We have found, working in different states, that the offer—or "Residential Contract of Sale"—is a bit different, but overall they contain the same information for your review. The contracts are straightforward after your property manager or real estate agent walks you through the contract and explains the different sections. We typically complete the different sections of a standard contract as follows:

- **Property:** Make sure the address is correct when you are submitting the offer—we have had times when this mistake was made and we had to fix the paperwork.
- **Purchase price:** Typically our first offer, at least 25% below our estimated value.
- **Payment terms:** We typically put a deposit of $500 down with the offer. When we started out, we believed that a larger deposit was better, but we've seen a lot of our offers go through with just a $500 deposit. To date, we have not lost a deposit; we always have a contingency that allows us to walk away if we decide it's not a good deal for us.
- **Date of settlement:** We only provide cash offers or have alternative financing (lines of credit) available for us when we need to move forward on a property. We use the date of settlement as a negotiation tool. If time is of the essence on a deal, we can close when the seller is ready to close. Make sure the closing date works for you in case you need to secure bank financing.
- **Financing contingency:** We typically offer no financing contingency. If you are getting a loan, then you need to provide your financing contingency information.
- **Appraisal:** If you are obtaining a loan, the bank will need to make an appraisal. If the property gets a low appraisal, below your offer price, you may need to renegotiate the offer.
- **Home inspection:** We recommend this for the first couple of properties you purchase.
- **Termite inspection:** We've only purchased one property where termites were discovered after purchase; the cost to fix the problem with warranty was around $800. We

recommend termite inspections for the properties you are about to purchase.

- **Radon, mold, or asbestos inspections:** Depending on the area where you're investing, we recommend that you consider these inspections. Especially if you are investing in an area that is damp, we recommend you do a mold inspection.
- **Inclusions/exclusions:** If you and the seller agree that some items, such as the range, fridge, or dishwasher, should be part of the house, make sure you look at this section. These should be checked as part of the offer.

MAKING AND NEGOTIATING THE OFFER

We typically look at different sections of the contract that will help us tailor the offer to our needs. When we submit an offer, our expectation is that if the seller counteroffers we have the opportunity to restructure the offer to include different contingencies or change any section of the offer. As an example, not long ago we placed an offer on a property. The property was an estate sale—the son-in law, who was the executor, had never visited the property he was selling. The property had been on the market for around six months. We did an informal inspection of the property, and our only unknown was the condition of the boiler. Our decision was to present an offer with no contingencies; we made a low offer that should allow us to cover any issues with the boiler. If we receive a counteroffer, based on the amount the seller is asking, we may include contingencies concerning the boiler in our negotiations. The offer was accepted with minor changes.

As we discussed earlier, you need to understand the seller's motivation to sell. Understanding the motivation to sell will help you determine the amount you want to offer, as well as the other terms of the offer. We have used a number of the variables in the contract as a part of the negotiation, including:

- **Time to close:** When we were financing the homes we were buying, we typically communicated all the information and the price to the bank and had everything ready to expedite the financing process. When we are making a cash offer, we can close based on the timeline of the seller. This has been as soon as twenty days or as long as five months.
- **Rent back:** Allow the owner to rent back the property for a time if they need to sell the house but their new location is not ready. We offer sellers the opportunity to sell now and rent back at a lower price than market rental. We factor that into the price.
- **Financing contingency:** Cash offers seem to help us close deals faster, especially if the seller has had a bad experience with a deal falling through because of financing.
- **Property condition:** The property's condition, as well as the estimated renovation cost, factor heavily in our offer. To explain our price, we have sometimes presented the seller's agent with a list of concerns or renovations that we need to do, and this has helped with negotiations.

Price and price justification can be an important part of the offer depending on who you are submitting the offer to. From our point of view, for any offer that you are going to present, you need to expect a counter offer and then have to negotiate through that counter offer. It is important to understand several variables regarding the offer at the time you are planning your offer. Depending on the property condition, market demand, as well as what information you can get from your agent on why the property is being sold, you can then formulate the offer. You can make a decision on whether you want to add inspection contingencies, etc., as part of your planning. With today's technology, you have free tools from sites like Zillow.com that will allow you to refine the property estimate, as well as understand what other properties ar in the area that you can use to show/explain the offer rationale. Our recommendation is any time you are looking to put an offer forward, share your rationale and use that as your baseline for negotiation. You should always be willing to walk away from a deal if the numbers do not make sense.

Market conditions, situations, risks and your investment goals are always changing. Over the years we have had to adjust our negotiation approach based on those factors and we are in a continuous learning process.

SUPPORTING THE LOCAL ECONOMY: USE LOCAL CLOSING AND TITLE COMPANIES

We have made it a point to work with local companies, including attorneys and insurance companies. In addition to helping the local economy, these resources also understand the local areas.

In one of our areas, we do most of our closing remotely. The attorneys know us and they have all the paperwork necessary for us to close remotely. This makes the process easier for us, and when we run into problems, our local attorneys know how to handle it. Having local attorneys who understand the history of the area and can help resolve issues truly helps. On one property we had to resolve issues with the property lines and needed to work with the local courts to correct information on the deed; for another property, we had to work through issues involving a change in address for the property we were purchasing. A new road had been built and the owner of the house changed the main entrance, and therefore the address he was using for the property. The property address that was on the listing closing contract was not the same as the deed to the property. The local lawyers worked through the issues and helped us close the deal on time.

THE HOME INSPECTION

We recommend that you get a home inspection when you purchase your first couple of properties and that you schedule the inspections at a time when both of you can walk through the property with the inspector to learn what he or she is looking for. This will help educate you about what to look for in the next property. If you are getting financing from the bank, you will need to get the property inspected.

If you are looking at a number of properties as part of your purchase, you should be making inspections as part of your offer to ensure that you are not making a mistake. You will only need to pay for the inspection on a property for which your offer has been accepted.

COUPLES' ACTION SUMMARY

Celebrate the closing of each property!

Once a deal is closed, you have a lot to be excited about; you are one step closer to your financial freedom. You also have a lot of work and planning that needs to be done in order to ensure you are moving forward with getting your property ready for rental.

If you have followed some of our recommendations, you should be ready to move forward with little stress—it should be enjoyable and you should make it an event that is fun for the whole family. We make sure that we plan extra activities for our family.

We have made a point of celebrating the closing of each property, as we know each property purchase brings us closer to our financial goal and strengthens our determination to stay the course and keep working until we achieve our goal. Different properties may introduce you to new people in new areas or in your existing investment areas. After you close on your property, we recommend that you make a list of all the people who were involved in helping you close on the property. Think of it as a baby shower, and thank people the way you would for coming to a shower.

We recommend that you celebrate the closing with your team partners—make it a point to thank them for their effort and support in making it happen. Many times we take the team to dinner or just ensure that we thank our business partners for working with us and making our investments a success.

Once in a while, we get a problem property that requires a lot of our attention and slows the process down, and at times this makes us question our approach. By supporting each other, we have been able to overcome situations like this and secure a positive outcome.

NOTES

TASKS

- [ ]
- [ ]
- [ ]
- [ ]
- [ ]
- [ ]
- [ ]
- [ ]
- [ ]

CHAPTER ELEVEN

GETTING IT RENTED

Getting the property rented at the right price is our ultimate goal

- Invest based on business decisions and not emotions
- Stick to what you know
- When you realize you have made a mistake, you need to be proactive in making the tough decisions to remedy the situation
- Hire slow, fire fast when dealing with both property managers and contractors
- You have to be ready to make your own decisions—ask for advice, then make the ultimate decision yourself
- Beware of auctions and high-pressure sales
- Never give up: where there is a will, there is a way

CONGRATULATIONS: HOW TO GET STARTED NOW THAT YOU HAVE THE KEYS

PATIENCE

Getting the property rented once it is tenant-ready requires a lot of patience. You need to ensure that you or the property management company is screening the tenants to ensure that they have the ability to pay the rent and the right credit history. A bad tenant can be very costly.

It is always exciting for us when we close on a property and it is finally ours. For us, doing the walk-through after we close is truly fun—it is typically a reflection of our hard work, since we invest our time and energy in each property we buy. It's enjoyable to talk about the changes we are actually going to make, and if we do it right it gets us closer to our financial goals and objectives. We never forget why we are investing—and once the property is bought, it's time to think from a business perspective.

When the property is ready to be rented—that is, all the renovations have been done—we always make it a point to do a property walk-through to look for the finishing touches and ensure all the work that we wanted has been done. We know that the first impressions of prospective tenants are important and we know that tenants have options in what property they decide to rent. We want to ensure that when we compete in the market we are not only competing on monthly rent, but on providing a property that our tenants can call home for a while, and they become long-term tenants.

PUTTING TRUST IN YOUR PROPERTY MANAGEMENT COMPANY

The property management company that you are working with should have a lot of experience managing properties and should understand what is needed in order to get the property ready to be rented. Assuming that the property management company was with you when you did the original inspections and helped in the estimation of the high-level budget, both you and the property management company should be ready to meet, walk through the property, review the plan, and start fresh.

Now that the property is yours and you know what you paid for the property in the end, you need to make decisions about the best renovation approach, with the possible rental income in mind. Your final renovation and improvements plan should revolve around the potential rental income coupled with what improvements will increase the value of the house in the long term. Your decisions about how to move forward will depend on the type of property you purchased. As an example, one of the properties we purchased was a double unit converted into a single house.

The original plan during the walk-through was to reconvert back to a two-unit and rent each unit for between $450 and $550, depending on how they were finalized. When we started looking at the house more closely and got a couple of estimates on some of the renovations, we realized that one of the boilers was shot, water and electric work was needed beyond our original estimate, and we would need an extra $10-15K to get the property fully rented as two units. We took a step back and asked what the property would bring in as a single home; we were told maybe $600-$700 as a single home. The renovation to make it a single unit was around $5K less than our original budget. We decided to keep the house a single unit and we invested some extra money to make it a truly nice property. After renovations, we ended up renting the property for $650 a month, a great investment. When we were all done, we'd paid around $45K for the property and it was appraised after all the work for over $75K. This property generated great monthly income and delivered a great return on investment.

You need to be open to adjusting your original plans and to understand who will be renting your property and what they can afford. Again, remember: it is all about a good investment.

The property management company can work with you closely to finalize what is needed to get the property ready for rental, as well as help you finalize the rental price, lease, local property registration, and inspections. In addition, the property management company can help you deal with different tenant requests—for example, we have a no-pets policy for our rentals, but we had one tenant that qualified and was truly interested in our property who wanted to bring a pet. The property manager recommended an additional pet deposit, as well as a monthly rental fee of $25-50 per month per pet. Depending on the property, this policy has allowed our tenants to have pets and still protected our investment in the long run.

UNDERSTANDING THE CONCEPT OF PROPERLY WINTERIZING A PROPERTY

One thing we pay attention to and try to work on with our tenants is managing the heating costs of the property. Heating costs that get out of control can make you lose a good tenant.

One of the properties that we purchased was a beautiful two-unit house. It was our first property with electric heat, and it had a shared water bill. We were somewhat reluctant to purchase the property but the numbers made sense and the property management company was pretty confident that they could rent each side for around $600 a month. The property was pretty rundown and we put a lot of sweat and effort into getting it into good shape. When we went to rent the property, the electric company warned prospective tenants that the property's electric bills during the winter were extremely high, and they recommended that people think twice about the cost of heating that property. After losing a couple of tenants for this reason, we decided to take action. We asked the property manager to get a specialist who could help winterize and weatherproof the property. This meant winterizing all the windows, the front door (in addition to adding a screen door), insulating the attic, and fixing a window in the attic. The cost of all the work on the two units was around $1,000. We had the bill and could show new tenants the steps we were taking to bring the heating costs down, and we told them that we would work with them if the heating bills were an issue. We are able to rent both units, one unit for $650 a month and the other for $600 a month.

We think you should be aware of the concept of winterizing/weatherproofing a property. Winterizing a property means shutting down all the water for the property and turning off all the electricity on the property. You might do this if you are not planning to work on a newly acquired property during the winter; you can save money on heating, water, and electricity until you are ready to start working on the property. This is an important option to consider if you have a property that uses oil heat, since this can be extremely costly in the winter. In addition, if you do not plan to work on the property and the property is vacant, if you do not winterize the property and something goes wrong in the heating system, the pipes can freeze, which will cost you a lot.

COUPLES' ACTION SUMMARY

No one is perfect—we have both made mistakes in learning this business. We have gotten stressed with each other, but in the end we are here for each other and we are each other's inner strength. Another one of our policies in dealing with real estate is that only one person is allowed to vent at a time; when one person vents, the other person listens, and vice versa.

- When you are planning your budget, you need to plan the budget against the actual property you are purchasing. If you have a high-level approach, make sure you are refining it against the actual property and not just working with estimations.

- You need to track your expenses on a monthly basis; losing sight of your expenses on a given property can be expensive. As part of your monthly process, you need to track and understand where you are in relation to your planned budget.

Another thing that you need to take into account is that dealing with tenants and getting your property rented right is very important. Patience is important when working to get a property rented. Ensuring that you or your property management company are doing the due diligence of background checks when renting a property is very important in order to reduce the long-term overhead cost of managing the property.

When we have a property vacant, we have a policy to follow up with the property management company on a weekly basis, and we try to visit the vacant property on a monthly basis and do a walk-through, discuss what potential tenants have said about the property, and work with the property management company to see what changes need to be made to improve our prospect of renting the property.

NOTES

NOTES

TASKS

CHAPTER TWELVE

TAX MANAGEMENT AND CONSIDERATIONS

Ensuring that your expenses are tracked and recorded in a timely manner can provide a huge savings at the end of year

- ✔ Track your expenses for tax reporting
- ✔ Develop a system to categorize your expenses; lack of organization can be very expensive
- ✔ Devise a simple system early on and refine as you grow your investments
- ✔ Investing in properties has tax advantages

HIRE A TAX ACCOUNTANT WITH REAL ESTATE INVESTING EXPERIENCE EARLY

> **TAX ACCOUNTANTS**
>
> If you have been filing your taxes using tax software or an accountant who is not experienced in supporting real estate investors, we strongly recommend you reassess your end-of-year filing approach. In our opinion, it is a complex process, both in terms of planning and tracking your expenses and in terms of ensuring that you file correctly. We schedule aside four to eight hours every month to ensure all our tax records are updated.

CJ has always used a tax accountant to do all our personal taxes. We hear that a lot of people use tax software to file taxes, but to be honest we never saw the downside of using a tax accountant. When we started out, the cost of using a tax accountant was around $100-$300—today it is higher, since we have so many properties. We believe in being frugal but we believe it's worth the money to have tax experts represent us. We have an excellent relationship with our tax accountants. Our current accountant has expertise in working with real estate investors like us.

The advice, personal attention, and time that was spent on us by our tax accountant has saved us a lot money, in terms of teaching us what is tax deductible and what we need to do in order to get prepared for end-of-year filing. As an example, if you invest in real estate, you will need to submit a Schedule E Supplemental Income and Loss statement as part of your end-of-year taxes. This needs to be submitted for each property that you own. You can take a quick look at what is involved by visiting www.IRS.gov and searching for the keyword "Schedule E." You will need to be able to classify and categorize your expenses according to the following schedule items:

- Advertising
- Auto and travel
- Cleaning and maintenance
- Commissions
- Insurance
- Legal and other professional fees
- Management fees
- Mortgage interest paid to banks, etc.
- Other interest
- Repairs
- Supplies
- Taxes
- Utilities

We truly recommend that you work with a tax accountant to maximize your tax benefits. It is critical that you have a process in place to capture and track all your receipts. The law requires that you have receipts or purchase orders for all your expenses related to your investment property.

INVESTMENT PROPERTIES AND TAXES: KEY BENEFITS

When we first started investing we did not truly understand the difference between filing taxes for a personal/primary residence and filing taxes related to our rental/investment properties. What became apparent to us is that you have to treat your investment property as a business. In short, any expense that is necessary to manage, maintain, or fund your property can be taken into account when filing your taxes, as you'll see on the IRS Schedule E.

The Internal Revenue Service advises that you keep detailed records of all rental-related activities, including receipts and invoices. All of this is reported on Schedule E, Supplemental Income and Loss.

There are several tax benefits associated with investment properties. As an investor, you can deduct most expenses related to your rental property. We are not tax accountants, and we recommend that you talk to your tax account for a full explanation of the benefits. Over the years we have developed a better understanding of the benefits and the importance of properly tracking all expenses. Here are some of the key benefits that we have observed from investing in rental properties:

- Depreciation: Our understanding of depreciation is that you can have a positive cash flow up to the amount of your yearly depreciation without owing any income taxes
- ☺ Deduction of different types of expenses from rental income (see Schedule E)
- $ Losses can be carried forward from year to year against your rental income
- You can deduct mileage when traveling to your rental property. If you enjoy travelling to the area that you are investing in, and you have to travel to the area on business, your travel to the area is tax deductible.

Again, please talk to your tax accountant since each person's situation is different—different rules and regulations exist based on your combined income, possible expenses, and other situations. Also, different states may have different laws than those we have encountered. In addition, it has been strongly recommended to us that we get full tax recommendation when it comes to selling a property. We have not researched that option, since our investments have been long term and we have only sold one property (and that was for a loss)—still, that loss had a tax benefit, according to our accountant.

GETTING READY FOR THE TAX-FILING PROCESS

For us, getting ready for tax filing is a monthly activity. In the past, we would just compile all the related receipts and credit card bills, as well as all the statements from our property management company. We would keep them all in a couple of folders and a number of boxes so as not to lose them. A month or two prior to tax time, we would spend two to four weeks working late nights trying to complete the spreadsheets we provide to our accountant. I would go through the credit card bills and try to find all the receipts associated with the credit card entries. We used two to three of our personal credit cards, so I had to go through all three different statements for the year. CJ would go through all the property management statements and receipts, as well as other statements, which meant working through each property one at a time.

I can assure you that after two years, and as the number of properties increased, this became a very unmanageable situation that created a lot of stress between us. Based on our experience, our recommendations is that you:

- Keep a travel log/diary of your business travel and activities
- Establish a mechanism to capture and store all your receipts as related to business or business travel
- Establish a bank account dedicated to your investment properties

- Establish a credit card that is dedicated to your investment properties
- Perform your tax accounting activities on a monthly basis
- Be very organized and make it very easy for your accountant to go through your records—this will save you time and money
- Utilize a software program that is specially designed to help landlords or investors manage the accounting process; we use online software to manage our records
- Do not procrastinate
- Be honest in your reporting

As we continue to grow, we are in the process of looking for a part-time accountant to help us on a monthly basis. The main reason we are hiring additional help is due to the number of properties that we own and the number of projects we have going on at the same time. It is important to us that we are paying attention to our expenses on a monthly basis. This matters since, in order for you to claim an expense on your tax returns, you need to ensure you have your receipts in order. If you have a major repair expense that was charged but you do not have receipts, you may not be able to claim that expense if you cannot prove it existed.

PROPERTY MANAGEMENT COMPANIES AND ACCOUNTING SOFTWARE

Neither of us has any background in accounting; our only experience in accounting is balancing our home budget. Ours was a huge learning curve in trying to understand the basics of accounting, and we had to develop our own methods to figure out how best to track and manage our expenses.

For us, one of the major advantages of opting to work with property management companies is that we started to receive monthly statements containing our expenses. Out of two property management companies, one provided us with a simple Excel spreadsheet with expenses and a copy of the receipts for each month, while the other company provided us with a categorized monthly statement along with the receipts. Since we were getting receipts from both companies, we had to come up with a mechanism to keep track of the statements, as well as to categorize our expenses. In addition, the second company's accounting system tracked the expenses of the property for the year. The fact that the second company had already categorized our expenses helped us understand how expenses are categorized, and we followed the same approach in categorizing our expenses across the board.

The property management companies allowed us to track the money they spent, but that was only a portion of the expenses we needed to track. Any other expenses, such as our travel expenses, our interest, our legal and accounting expenses, as well as any other supplies or repairs related to the property, were not tracked. We needed to have an accounting approach that captured the expenses from all aspects of the business.

The options we looked at included:

- Manual tracking
- Excel spreadsheet
- QuickBooks
- Online property management software

When we started we had heard that QuickBooks was the tool to use to manage your expenses. We purchased the QuickBooks Simple Start edition, figuring that it would be easy to use and we would be up and running in no time. To our disappointment we were not able to figure out how to tailor the application to our needs. In reading more about this online, we realized that you need to customize the application for it to work for a property investment businesses, and we might need to hire an accountant to help us with that customization. We did not want to invest hundreds of dollars in setting up an accounting system we weren't even sure would serve our needs.

In order to address the short-term need, CJ developed a spreadsheet to track our expenses based on information in the IRS Schedule E and the property management company's categorized expense report. We used the spreadsheet until we had five properties.

With five properties, completing the spreadsheets started to become a challenge. At that time, CJ started looking into other options. We were able to find a number of online software programs designed to help investors like us manage rental properties. One of the main things that we were looking for in an online tool was something that could help us track the profit and loss on each property, the ability to get a consolidated report that provided a report on all of our properties, and—the most important criteria—a tool that could generate the Schedule E for us for all our properties. After looking at a number of different tools and trying several, we were able to find the right program for us, and we have been using it for a number of years. Our tax accountant also likes the organization and the reports we provide at the end of the year. The beauty of the online tool is that you can access the tool from anywhere and update it as needed. The only disadvantage we find in using tools of this kind is that they are not as fast as using a spreadsheet, so we just plan to spend a bit more time working with it. Importantly, the capabilities of the software tool and its scalability to manage a larger number of properties have allowed us to continue growing our investments without having to change tools.

COUPLES' ACTION SUMMARY

Track your expenses and ensure you hire a good accountant.

Tracking expenses and ensuring that you are capturing all the information needed to update the books and get ready for end-of-year taxes requires discipline and attention to detail.

Tax management is a very important aspect of managing your finances. Failure to pay your taxes can be very expensive in the long run. In addition, as your number of properties grows, it will become harder to manage your taxes if you are not organized and don't have a process in place to track and manage your expenses. It is important that both of you understand what needs to be managed in terms of taxes and accounting records.

We truly recommend that you schedule time early on in your investment activities to meet with your tax advisor or accountant. We strongly recommend that both of you be present at the meeting and that the meeting be face to face. We recommend having your accountant walk you through a list of all the documents you need to have ready by the end of the year in order to do your taxes. For example, when you close on a property, you need to ensure you provide your accountant with the HUD statement. In addition, our recommendation is to have your accountant explain how to itemize and categorize your expenses. The more organized you are, the less time it will take for your accountant to finalize your taxes. This will reduce your overall cost.

COUPLES' ACTION SUMMARY

Once you develop an understanding of the tax-filing procedures, it is important to work as a team and to support each other in making sure you are keeping track of everything. In splitting the work, we work with each other and take turns being responsible for capturing all the receipts on each trip. We recommend that you plan some time together to go through your expenses on a monthly basis.

On our web site, www.TheHappyCouplesGuide.com, we provide links to tools that we recommend for managing your expenses, as well as accounting tools that make it easier for you to manage and track your records.

NOTES

TASKS

23

CHAPTER THIRTEEN

A NOTE ABOUT DEALING WITH TENANTS

Let your property management company manage your tenants—it is a tough job

- Tenants are your primary customers—they pay your bills, and we do not forget that
- Communicate to your tenants the support system you have put in place to meet their needs
- The head of the support system is the property management company
- Even if you are called directly, your first action is to reach out to your property management company
- Do not build a relationship with your tenants if you do not plan on supporting them personally—let your property management company manage your tenants for you
- Do not provide your contact information to your tenants; all calls should go through the property management company

TENANTS

BE PROACTIVE

We have found that when you run into issues with a tenant not being compliant with the lease, either by missing payments or any other situation, it's best to engage immediately and deal with the situation with a strong adherence to the lease terms. Do not wait to take action to remedy the situation.

Dealing with tenants can be challenging, especially as you acquire more properties. We have mentioned that we believe that our tenants are our customers. The term customer may have implications that "the customer is always right," but that is not what we mean by it. We treat our tenants as customers that have to abide by specific laws and rules. As long as they are following the rules and lease terms, things are great; if not, then the situation must be managed, the same way that when someone leases a car, they are treated with courtesy and respect at all times, but if issues arise, then the situation must be addressed. You need to ensure you treat all your tenants the same and follow the same approach with all of them. Your time and effort in dealing with and supporting your tenants will dramatically increase if you have an issue that needs to be resolved immediately.

As we mentioned before, having the right property management company in place can help you resolve a lot of your issues, but at times the property management company cannot make decisions and they will reach out to you for a recommendation. You need to provide leadership and guidance to your property management company in regards to how you want them to deal with any given situation. It is important that you support your tenants equally. If a tenant gets your contact information and starts reaching out to you directly, you cannot ignore the situation, but you need to get your property management company involved. Do not deal with the issue personally—you need to keep your property management company involved, as that is why you hired them. If the property management company is not able to deal with the issue, you need to work with their management to remedy the situation.

You have invested a lot of hard-earned money into your property. Our philosophy is that your tenants will take as much care of your property as you do of them. We consider ourselves to be in the service industry, and we work hard to keep our tenants happy and with us for the long term.

In addition, as a landlord/real estate investor, you have to be ready to deal with emergencies as they come up. The property manager is the first line of communication, but the property manager will need your approval to make a lot of decisions as they relate to your properties. Over the past twelve years, we have been lucky that we not have had any major issues, but it is something that is always on our minds, and we have to ensure that we provide professional, quick, and timely support to our property managers. One of the issues we had to deal with was a driver falling asleep behind the wheel of a car and running into the porch of one of our properties. Thankfully no one was hurt, but we had to deal with the situation quickly and make decisions to ensure our tenants had access to the property and the repairs were dealt with in a timely and professional manner. We were very lucky that we had a great property manager who managed the situation for us, and she helped us make the right decisions to properly take care of our tenants.

DEALING WITH CHALLENGING TENANTS

From our experience renting properties, we have realized that the majority of tenants are great people. We have had our challenges with a number of tenants over the years, and when you have a problem, it can escalate and become very challenging. We have also found out that different states have different laws, and these laws, in our opinion, are either investor-friendly or tenant-friendly. For example, we believe that Maryland and Pennsylvania are investor-friendly, while New York is tenant-friendly. That is, each state has specific laws about how to deal with tenants who are not paying the rent or who break the lease agreement. You need to ask your property manager to explain the local laws about dealing with a tenant and ensure you understand them when choosing where to invest.

Please be aware that tenants have rights, and that their rights and your rights are protected by the terms of the lease that you have in place. When you have a problem with a tenant, your lease is an important tool. Working with an established property management company most probably means having a strong tenant selection process, as well as a strong lease in place that addresses local laws.

Challenges with tenants can include—but are certainly not limited to—tenants not paying the rent on time, bad checks, having more people than the lease allows living on the property, having pets without permission, and/or noise disturbance. We have tried to deal with these challenges ourselves in the past, but today we mostly leave it to our property managers, who seem to be experts in dealing with these challenges. They also truly understand the lease and the local laws, and they know how best to deal with these kinds of problems. It is our experience that once you start having problems with a certain tenant, they will not just go away by themselves—we have learned that when an issue comes up, you need to work with your property management to address it sooner rather than later.

During one of CJ's travels, he met with a real estate investor who has four properties, and they started talking about their investments. One of the challenges she talked about was collecting the rent from a bad tenant and eventually getting the tenant off of the property—the investor indicated that in the end she had to pay the tenant to vacate the property. We have heard this from multiple people, and in the past, prior to working with property management companies, we had similar experiences. Dealing with tenants can be very tough. If you are going to do it yourself you need to be organized and understand your local laws so that you are ready to address issues when they come up. In addition, if you plan to manage yourself, you need to prepare for the possibility of having more vacancies and a higher turnover rate for tenants.

COUPLES' ACTION SUMMARY

Be courteous and treat everyone with respect, even in tough situations—it is just business. Make sure your property management company does not provide your direct contact information to any of your tenants, and let them deal with situations that arise. If you have to deal with the tenants directly, work as a team and ensure you are managing the situation in a professional manner. Regardless of what the situation is, as soon as you lose your temper or lose control of the situation it will get harder to manage the outcome. It will take a team to deal with a tough tenant.

- Listen and try to understand the situation
- ? Ensure the situation does not get defensive or argumentative
- ☺ Be honest, do not make excuses, and work to resolve the issue even if you made a mistake, e.g. you did not fix something that has been broken for a while
- Ensure you do not raise your voice when communicating
- ✔ Be understanding, and be willing to put yourself in the tenants' shoes and work to resolve the issue; be supportive

If the issue is due to late payments, you will need to work with the tenant and put a plan of action together to ensure they pay you. Be proactive. If all else fails, you need to take more assertive legal action.

continued

COUPLES' ACTION SUMMARY

We have discussed these issues with our property managers; each one of them has a system for dealing with tenants who do not pay on time. One of our property managers has a policy that if a tenant is fifteen days late paying the rent, they will go ahead and submit all the papers to start the eviction process. They have requested that we have a budget in place to support this process—the cost is minimal, and this policy has been very effective for ensuring tenants are paying the rent: tenants who do not plan to pay the rent will be out sooner rather than later. We have had incidents in which this property manager worked with tenants to pay over months, but the submitted paperwork forced the tenant to actively work with the property manager in order to address the situation.

Having a plan and establishing an approach with your property manager for how to deal with a problem tenant will help reduce a lot of stress in the future and will make managing your rental properties a more enjoyable experience.

NOTES

NOTES

TASKS

CHAPTER FOURTEEN

A NOTE ABOUT WORKING WITH CONTRACTORS

Dealing with contractors can be challenging—be ready and be organized

- Ensure you have a budget prior to engaging contractors
- You need to be organized and have a detailed list of tasks that you expect your contractors to complete
- If you are not local to the job, let your property management company manage your renovations
- Not paying close attention and conducting regular inspections of your renovation can lead to a lot of surprises, lost revenue, and lost time to market

CONTRACTORS: MAKE SURE YOU HAVE A COMMUNICATED BUDGET

DOCUMENT

When dealing with contractors, make sure you document and write down what was agreed upon. This should include the work order, as well as the budget and timeline for completion of the work. Failure to do so can lead to a lot of challenges.

Even though you may be able to get a great deal on the purchase price for a property, you have to ensure you manage the renovation on time and on budget. Our major challenge in most of our renovation projects has been managing our budgets and ensuring that the work being delivered meets our standards and expectations.

Most of our investment properties are located at least a two-and-a-half-hour drive away, so we can't visit the property being renovated often. We plan visits as frequently as possible during the renovation and rely on our property management company for regular updates. Both of us have day jobs and family responsibilities and activities over the weekends that sometimes make it harder for us to travel on a regular basis to check on the progress. We have made sure that we keep our weekends open during renovation periods and visit the area as often as possible.

If we have to give a word of advice, it would be to expect changes and modifications to the original budgets as the job progresses. You have to communicate and agree on a budget prior to start of the job; you need to set expectations and parameters if a specific issue is found that would affect the budget. If you do not have that in place, you should not even start a renovation. If you are working with a new contractor, break the job into multiple budgets and tasks and give out one task at a time. This will allow you to make decisions to replace the contractor in case you encounter difficulties. In addition, we recommend that you be as specific as possible about your goals for the renovation. It is important not to change direction in the middle of the work due to personal preferences—you may need to change plans due to certain issues being discovered, but you should try to stick to the original plan as much as possible if you want to stay on budget.

Besides budget, the other important factor you need to ensure is communicated to any contractors is the timeframe in which the project needs to be completed. Since each month the house is not rented you are losing money or the cost of rental, it is important that the contractor understands that delays in the timeframe incur other costs beyond just paying for the cost of construction. Sometimes when we've run into new issues, we have forgone other planned renovations or taken shortcuts on other aspects of the work that were not critical in order to stay on schedule. In addition, when you are working to define the timeframe it will take to complete the work, you may get an estimate that it will take fifteen days to get the job done; you should not assume that this is fifteen consecutive days. You need to decide on a planned start date and a planned end date, and ensure that your project is scheduled for specific days in between, as the contractor may have a couple of projects running in parallel.

T & M VS. FIXED COST

After a lot of renovations, we have learned the hard way to only go with fixed-cost proposals rather than time-and-material (T&M) projects. One of the main factors behind this statement is that everything we do has to be budget-based. Any time we have gone with T&M projects we have not been able to manage our budgets. In a T&M project, you really need to be able to visit the property being renovated on a regular basis. If you are able to do this and you can see the progress on a daily basis, it is okay to go with a T&M project. If you are far away from your investment property, and you do not have a contractor with a proven track record whom you trust fully, then we do not recommend accepting a T&M proposal.

One of our projects was a real learning experience about T&M projects. We had a new contractor whom we had not worked with, but who came highly recommended by our current contractor. Our current contractor was overloaded and we would have had to wait some time before getting started on our renovation. The new contractor only worked on a T&M basis and we agreed to a detailed work order with budget and expected time. We broke the work into multiple tasks in order to see the work quality and time of delivery. The work quality was good, but he missed all planned dates and we were struggling with deciding how to move forward, as we were already a couple of weeks behind schedule. We started to increase our daily visits to the site. It turned out that the team was taking two to four trips to the hardware store per day, they were missing equipment or would drive to a different job site to exchange equipment, and one of the guys we were paying to do actual work was just managing the team and drinking coffee all day. He had no motivation to finish the work early, since his team was paid on a T&M basis. To make a long story short, we ended our relationship within a week, since he was not able to produce a project plan to finish the work and convert the work from T&M to fixed price. If he had been willing to convert to a fixed price we would have continued working with him, because we did like his work. We got someone else to finish the work at a fixed price and moved on.

We have made it a policy to always ask the property manager to get us three bids on major work even though we know the contractors that they use and we trust their work. This has helped us stay competitive in managing budgets. At times we are surprised by the wide range of cost variance, especially coming from contractors that have done a lot of work for us. This does not mean that you always have to go with the lowest bid, but it provides you grounds to negotiate the price and bring the price down if needed. We do not do T&M-based projects anymore.

COUPLES' ACTION SUMMARY

Be in charge, and empower your property management company to manage the situation.

The more details you provide about what needs to be done and the more planning you do upfront, the more you'll save on any project.

It is important that as a couple you are communicating and know exactly what needs to be done on a project when you are working with contractors. We always make it clear to the different contractors who has the final decision on a given project and who they take direction from. This way, we do not have contractors trying to play a game with us. We typically divide this responsibility across different projects as needed. Our objective is to get the job done on time and on budget. Make sure that you are taking the time to sit down, talk about each project, and share your thoughts about it.

As a couple, you need to decide who will be responsible for follow-up with contractors on ongoing renovation projects. The decision about what needs to be done should be a joint decision, but we typically divide the responsibilities of who is following up with the contractor and who is keeping an eye on the current investments and other tasks that need to be managed. It is important that you empower and trust each other in working to get things done. At times we even split the work of who is working with what property manager for a given period of time. We try to continue to balance our daily work activities, as well as our investment tasks. As an example, since I'm in sales, the last month of the quarter is typically a hectic month for me; CJ typically manages all investment activities, or we slow things down during that time to ensure we can focus on our day jobs and that we continue to be successful at what we do.

NOTES

TASKS

CHAPTER FIFTEEN

MODIFYING OUR APPROACH AND ONLINE RESOURCES

Start investing in a way that works for you

- Different geographical locations may offer different home prices
- We are confident that if you look within four hours' driving distance from where you live you will find properties within your budget that fit our formula
- Planning and willingness to move forward and invest in real estate is key: where there is a will, there is a way

MODIFYING OUR APPROACH TO FIT YOUR STYLE AND CONDITIONS

MEET YOUR NEEDS

Take the time to go through the basic calculations recommended in this chapter. They will help you develop a long-term strategy and better understand your current position. Review and discuss the results of your calculations together.

The approach we describe has worked for us, but it may not fit your current lifestyle. We understand that properties in different areas will have different prices, and we understand that no one approach fits the need of everyone. What we have tried to do in this book is provide you with an overview of how we stabilized our financial position, eliminated our bad debt and put a plan to invest into action. The plan and approach that we have put in place has been successful for us. If you follow our approach to stabilize your financials and plan for your future, we believe you will be in a better financial position in the future.

MODIFYING YOUR APPROACH

When modifying our approach to meet your needs, you can adjust the ROI calculations and the time it would take to recoup your current investment. The concepts that we stand behind fully are: finding the right area to invest in, planning for your future, controlling your spending, using all your tools in negotiations, finding good deals, working with property managers, and taking your time growing your investment. You need to be conservative in your approach and put a plan in place that works for you.

As we mentioned earlier, our investment formula was based on wanting to try and achieve the following objectives:

- Having a target goal on the supplemental monthly income that we'd need every year after retiring
- Recouping our financial investments and eliminating our mortgage debt on our investment properties in five to seven years, period
- Ensuring the properties we purchase will have a high ROI when we sell them in the future

BASIC MATH/FUNCTIONS TO HELP YOU PLAN

(A) Monthly Income Needed = ((Yearly Income 1 + Yearly Income 2) /12) x .8

(B) Monthly Income Per Property = Average monthly rent x (.65)

(C) Number of Properties Needed = Monthly Income needed / Monthly Income per property

(D) Years to Achieve Goal = Number of properties Needed / Properties to Acquire per year

(E) Cash Investment Needed = Average Price per Property x Number of properties needed

(F) Yearly Savings for Investment Needed = Cash investment needed / Years to achieve goal

(G) Current Ability to Invest = Savings per Year / Average Price per Property

(H) Years to Pay Off Property = Outstanding balance / Yearly principle payment

The above calculations are based on the following assumptions:

- Both couples are working.
- Only 80% of current income will be needed after retirement. Hopefully you will be debt and mortgage free by the time you are ready to retire.
- Monthly income from property assumes a conservative approach. It assumes that 35% of monthly income is allocated for property expenses, as well as taking into account some vacancies every year.
- Average price per property includes closing cost as well as other costs to acquire the property.
- You have calculated what is realistic in terms of your yearly savings. For us, as a couple, today we assume one of our incomes will be used 100% for investment while we will live on the other income.

If you plan on purchasing properties over the next five to fifteen years as part of your long-term investment strategy, you will have a number of properties that are producing income. In addition, if by that time all your properties are paid off, your monthly expenses to manage each property should be low. If you followed our approach your income from the properties could be from:

- Rental income: Your rental income from each property
- Property value: Each property is like a fund; you can keep, you can sell, or you can take a partial loan against it to get the income you need

In addition to our rental income, you may have income from other savings, including:

- 401(k) savings and returns
- Social Security
- Other investment income/holdings

Now that you have an understanding of our basic mathematical formulas, as well as your current savings, you need to figure out how to tailor our formula and approach to fit your needs. You will also need to be patient, since we recommend you start slowly and only accelerate the process once you have learned the ropes. You can always revisit your approach every year and adjust your plans and objectives. What is important is that you develop an initial approach. The calculations mentioned in the following section reference the basic calculations table earlier in this chapter.

STEPS

Step 1: Develop an understanding of your financials and what steps are needed to reduce your debt, etc. You need to be able to get an idea of how much you can save per year.

Step 2: Develop an understanding of your monthly income goals in the future. You can use Formula (A).

Step 3: Develop an understanding of the property values in the different areas where you want to invest.

Step 4: Develop an understanding of the rental income in the different areas where you want to invest.

Step 5: Perform an analysis on the different areas where you plan to invest based on the information gathered in Steps 2-4. This will help you understand what is realistic based on your current financial situation and what you need to do to plan for the future.

- Calculate monthly income for the different areas – Formula (B)
- Calculate number of properties needed – Formula (C)
- Calculate cash investment needed – Formula (E)
- Calculate yearly savings needed – Formula (F)

Step 6: Based on the information gathered in Step 5, you can make decisions about how you want to proceed and develop a formula that will work for your plans.

When we looked at these numbers, we realized that we needed to explore areas outside our neighborhood but within a couple of hours drive in order to be able to achieve our objectives.

ONLINE RESOURCES

We have developed a number of online resources that support this book and will provide you with more information, tools, and links to help expand on the topics we've covered. You can find us on the web at this link:

TheHappyCouplesGuide.com

A FINAL NOTE

We are sure that with self-confidence and determination you will be able to achieve success. Our strategy is a long-term strategy with defined goals that work for us, and we are sure it will also work for you even if you do not follow our formula exactly. If things change in the future, you can sell one of the investment properties you bought at a bargain price to help deal with a difficult situation. You have the opportunity to challenge yourselves, to have fun, and to invest in your future. We assure you it will feel great as you start acquiring one property after the other, get them managed, and then move on to the next property. Life moves at such a fast pace, if you come up with a plan and just work through it, you will be surprised by how many properties you may come to own in the next five or six years and the returns that you can start seeing from them. Make sure you make it fun.

On our journey through life, we are surprised by how many people think like us and want to invest in real estate for their future; they all believe in self-made successes. If you look at successful people around you that have had to make it on their own, they invested smartly and worked through every situation to build their future. All we've provided is an approach—before you really get going, you need to set your own goals and believe that through planning and execution, one step at a time, you can achieve them. We have always believed that by working together as a couple we can make a difference in the world around us, and this was one of the driving factors behind our decision to write this book and share our experiences with you.

We hope that by reading this book we have inspired you to plan your trips, explore investment areas around you, and start on the path to your financial freedom. We want to wish you the best, and we hope that like us you will be excited about the adventure, and that you will work together as a couple not only to strengthen your financial position, but to strengthen your relationship and to become closer to each other. May you succeed and achieve all that you plan and hope for. We leave you with an Irish blessing:

May the road rise up to meet you.
May the wind be always at your back.
May the sun shine warm upon your face.,
and rains fall soft upon your fields.
And until we meet again,
May God hold you in the palm of His hand.

NOTES

TASKS

- ☐
- ☐
- ☐
- ☐
- ☐
- ☐
- ☐
- ☐
- ☐

ABOUT THE HAPPY COUPLES GUIDES

The Happy Couples Guide (TheHappyCouplesGuide.com) series is designed to provide a practical, comprehensive guide that can be easily implemented by working individuals, especially couples who are both working. The series is designed to provide insight and lessons learned from other couples.

The Happy Couples Guide concept is creating books and stories that are motivational and geared toward taking life lessons and providing the mechanisms to share these life stories and experiences with others. The series is intended to share with you how couples can leverage each other's strengths and divide up roles and responsibilities to make it work.

As we move forward and take the series to the next level, we hope to bring forth exciting titles that focus on original content in all formats with the mission to educate, entertain, and inspire readers for generations.

May we recommend you get a copy of our books for each one of you; the book is designed such that you can track your notes and tasks at the end of each chapter. The book can be utilized as a planning guide to capture your notes and tasks as you read through the series, ultimately helping you build a better future for you and your family.

If you enjoyed this book, we hope you'll take the time to take a look at some of the other great books from the Happy Couples Guides

The Happy Couples Guide to Selling Your Home

answers the question, "Once you do decide to sell your home, and you know the reasons why, what's next?" Chakib and Jinan walk you through each step, as well as through the numerous emotional struggles and challenges you might encounter.

Throughout the helpful guide, the authors share their experiences and lessons learned in selling homes. They provide a comprehensive planning guide with easy-to-follow steps, each designed to help you in making your house stand out in the crowd. Their goal is to help you sell your house fast and get the best offers. med decisions of where and how to best invest your own hard-earned money.

The Happy Couples Guide to Buying Your First Home

is designed for reading early in the home buying process, even prior to engaging with a real estate agent, and to refer to again and again. Planning and buying your home can be an extremely stressful and challenging process. This guide will help you define your family needs, provide an easy-to-follow process, highlight the Pros and Cons of using a real estate agent, present recommendations and interview questions for choosing an agent, and compile negotiation strategies to help you throughout the buying process.

The Happy Couples Guide to Planning Your Child's College Admission Process

empowers parents and caregivers in getting a head start in supporting, and planning their child's college admissions process from early childhood to high school. Designed as a workbook, it can be personalized for your child allowing you to capture information over the years that will be needed as part of the application process.

The book is divided into four sections to support you and your child through this journey: Getting Ready, Components of a Successful Admissions Application, Financing, and a Bonus Section with information on how a working couple can save money to support their children's education.

The Happy Couples Guide to Homemade Cheeses & Yogurt

provides simple and easy to follow recipes that you can use in your own kitchen to make fresh cheeses and yogurt for your family. Over the years, we have enjoyed yogurt and cheese produced by Jinan's dad, master cheese maker Ziad Jaber, who has a Master of Science degree in Animal Science and Dairy Production and had his own dairy farm. The process is straightforward. Once you master the basics steps, you can have fun and experiment with the process and varieties to create your own unique and flavorful cheeses and yogurts.

Made in United States
North Haven, CT
27 September 2023

42054271R00143